THE G U

TRUTH UNDER ATTACK

VOLUME 2

Cults and sects

DR ERYL DAVIES

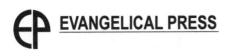

EVANGELICAL PRESS

EVANGELICAL PRESS
Faverdale North Industrial Estate, Darlington, DL3 0PH, England

Evangelical Press USA
P. O. Box 825, Webster, New York 14580, USA

e-mail: sales@evangelicalpress.org
web: www.evangelicalpress.org

First published 2005

British Library Cataloguing in Publication Data available

ISBN 0 85234 587 9

Printed and bound in Great Britain by Creative Print & Design Wales, Ebbw Vale, South Wales.

CONTENTS

Section F: Established cults

Postscript: Summary of major Bible doctrines

INTRODUCTION AND OUTLINE OF THE THREE-VOLUME SERIES

For over three decades I have researched the complex subject of cults and new religious movements. My reasons for doing so have been three-fold.

Firstly, in the context of evangelism I met increasing numbers of people belonging to the cults. In sharing the gospel of grace with them I found it helpful to acquaint myself with their teaching. Evangelism, therefore, has always been for me a primary reason for researching this subject.

Secondly, but closely related, was the fact that my own church members were often confused as a result of talking to cult members who called at their homes or approached them in shopping areas. Here was a challenge to instruct Christians more adequately in the Scriptures and also to mobilize them in personal evangelism.

A third reason for continuing this research, especially in recent years, has been the regular requests for help from missionaries, pastors and individual Christians troubled by cult activities in their situations. On occasions, some have been distressed over the involvement in a cult by a close relative or even infiltration of a Bible-believing church by cult members thus causing division and confusion.

This series, originally published in two editions in 1990 and 1995, has undergone major revision, updating and expansion with several new groups included. Volume 1 was published in 2004 and volume 3 is to follow. An outline of all three volumes is included below. The series is intended to provide Christians, churches, schools and colleges with a reliable introduction to, and overview of, the contemporary Western cult scene from a biblical perspective.

Whether you are a Christian, a searcher or a cult member, I appeal to you to read regularly and understand 'the holy Scriptures, which are able to make you wise for salvation through faith in Christ Jesus' (2 Timothy 3:15).

Volume 1: Deviations from biblical Christianity

Introduction to the three-volume series

Section A: Deviations from biblical Christianity in Trinitarian churches/movements

1. Worldwide Church of God
2. Seventh-Day Adventists
3. Protestant churches: modernism and post-modernism

4. Roman Catholicism
5. Quakers: the Religious Society of Friends
6. Exclusive Brethren: 'Taylorites'
7. International Church of Christ
8. A Nameless Group: 'Go-Preachers'
9. New Apostolic Church
10. Universal Pentecostal Church
11. The United Church of God
12. Horst Schaffranek
13. William Branham
14. Moral Re-Armament
15. Faith Movement

Section B: Unitarian churches and movements

16. Unitarian churches
17. The Way International
18. 'Jesus-only': the Apostolic Oneness movement
19. Where are today's Arians?
20. Jehovah's Witnesses
21. Christadelphians

Section C: Personal and pastoral challenges

22. Personal and pastoral challenges

Postscript: Summary of major Bible doctrines

OUTLINE

VOLUME 2: CULTS AND SECTS

Section D: What are cults and sects?

Chapters in this section are more reflective and basic. One important reason for this is that it is essential to understand terms like 'sect', 'cult' and 'new religious movements' and also to appreciate how and why they are used. I indicate my preference for using the term 'cult'.

Features which are common to cults are also identified and illustrated before I suggest some criteria for recognizing a cult. This is particularly important and useful because cults are now a worldwide problem. For reasons which will be apparent in chapter 5 and also in the following section, some national governments are worried over the cults phenomena and the potential for further, possibly national, tragedies. The example of the UK government and one of its security agencies, MI5, is used to highlight this aspect.

Section E: Case studies and issues arising

Two case studies are undertaken in this section. While the two cults studied here are different in terms of their background and impact, the UK and USA governments believed both could pose a threat to society. In the case of Waco, the threat was realized in a tragic way. These studies will teach us some important and practical lessons.

Section F: Established cults

All the cults included in this section are what we call 'established' cults. In other words, they have been active for well over fifty years, some much longer. Their names and activities may be reasonably well known to you. You may even have met a Mormon missionary or seen some Rastafarians in your area. Perhaps, too, a Scientologist may have tried to recruit you on to one of their courses. You really do need to know about these 'established' cults.

Postscript: Summary of major Bible doctrines

VOLUME 3: PAGANISM AND THE NEW SPIRITUALITIES

Section G: Revelation

1. Real Revelation and Relationality
2. Redemptive and Restorative Revelation

Section H: Paganism and the New Spiritualities

3. The New Spiritualities: varied and popular
4. The New Spiritualities: criteria for testing them
5. The New Spiritualities: more criteria
6. Evangelical Spirituality: background
7. Evangelical Spirituality: biblical and historical
8. Paganism: the contemporary scene

9. Paganism: the background
10. Paganism: beliefs
11. Paganism and evangelicals

Section I: Spiritistic groups

12. The occult: an overview and warning
13. Hallowe'en
14. Spiritism
15. Theosophy
16. Eckenkar: the ancient art of Soul-Travel
17. Anthroposophy (Rudolf Steiner Movement)
18. Satanism: introduction and outline
19. Satanism: a case study

Section J: Eastern movements

20. New Age movement
21. Baha'i
22. Hare Krishna: International Society for Krishna Consciousness
23. Yoga
24. Transcendental Meditation
25. Elan Vital (formerly Divine Light Mission)
26. Osho (formerly Rajneesh Foundation)

Section K: Self-improvement groups

27. EST: Erhard Seminars Training
28. Exegesis

HOW TO USE *THE GUIDE*

This is the second volume in the *Truth under attack* trilogy, which has been revised and updated for the popular series called *The Guide*. This series covers books of the Bible on an individual basis, such as *Colossians and Philemon*, and relevant topics such as *Christian comfort*. The series' aim is to communicate the Christian faith in a straightforward and readable way.

Each book in *The Guide* will cover a book of the Bible or topic in some detail, but will be contained in relatively short and concise chapters. There will also usually be questions at the end of each chapter for personal study or group discussion, to help you to study the Word of God more deeply.

An innovative and exciting feature of *The Guide* is that it is linked to its own web site. As well as being encouraged to search God's Word for yourself, you are invited to ask questions related to the book on the web site, where you will not only be able to have your own questions answered, but also be able to see a selection of answers that have been given to other readers. The web site can be found at www.evangelicalpress.org/

TheGuide. Once you are on the site you just need to click on the 'select' button at the top of the page, according to the book on which you wish to post a question. Your question will then be answered either by Michael Bentley, the web site co-ordinator and author of *Colossians and Philemon*, or others who have been selected because of their experience, their understanding of the Word of God and their dedication to working for the glory of the Lord.

Many other books have already been published in this series. These include *The Bible book by book*, *Job*, *Judges*, *Ecclesiastes*, *Esther*, *Revolutionary forgiveness* and *Christian comfort;* many more will follow. It is the publisher's hope that you will be stirred to think more deeply about the Christian faith, and will be helped and encouraged in living out your Christian life, through the study of God's Word, in the difficult and demanding days in which we live.

THE GUIDE

Section D:

WHAT ARE CULTS AND SECTS?

THE GUIDE

CHAPTER ONE

REFLECTIONS: THE TERM 'SECT'

A BRIEF HISTORY

A number of readers have responded in recent years to what I have written on the cults. These responses have often been positive but some have been critical. Underlying these critical responses, one detects a feeling of hurt and even disgust that their group has been described as a cult or as possessing cultic characteristics. I understand their sense of pain. That is to be expected, for members of cults naturally see themselves quite differently.

Key terms

This is the context in which I am going to pause and reflect. Consequently, we will now consider terms such as 'sect', 'cult' and 'new religious movement' (abbreviated to NRM). These are key terms, which are traditionally used to refer to groups like Jehovah's Witnesses, the Moonies or the Family of Love.

But how are these terms being used today? What do they mean? Which term, if any, should we employ? The answers, I am afraid, are somewhat complex, but let me explain and consider them separately. I confine myself in this chapter to the term 'sect'.

Sect

For sociologists like Professor Bryan R. Wilson the term 'sect' is preferable to that of 'cult' or 'NRM'. There appear to be three reasons at least for this.

Firstly, they regard it as a neutral term; it neither condemns a group nor assesses its teaching in a judgemental manner. With this usage there are no unfavourable innuendos or associations. It really is a harmless yet useful term for sociologists.

Secondly, in this way, the term 'sect' assumes an exclusively social significance. For example, there are specific social factors and changes in society that facilitate the emergence, appeal and demise of sects. This will be illustrated later. But I want to underline here the fact that in using the term 'sect' sociologists are seeking to describe and understand the phenomenon from a social perspective alone. They are not interested in deciding whether the teaching is biblical or not.

Long history

Thirdly, for sociologists the term 'sect' has a long and varied history. The point is well made. They remind us that sects have appeared at regular intervals in the history of the church, especially since the sixteenth-century Protestant Reformation. For example, some groups in Martin Luther's time were wildly excitable, charismatic and even irresponsible. Yet, later, the Congregationalists, Baptists, Quakers and others were often regarded as sects posing a threat to both church and state.

In the eighteenth century the Methodists also tended to be viewed as a sect. According to sociologists, sects such as Jehovah's Witnesses, Mormons and Christadelphians, which emerged in the second part of the nineteenth century, also fit into this historical pattern of deviant groups.

For these three reasons, then, sociologists tend to use the term 'sect' but they do so in a neutral way.

Advantages

There are advantages in using the word 'sect' in these ways and we will mention two of them here. Firstly, as stated above, sociologists are expressing neutrality and tolerance through the use of this term. Indeed, they can be viewed as encouraging religious freedom by their neutrality. This is commendable in our religiously pluralist society, consistent with Christian 'charity' and in accord with the European Convention on Human Rights (in particular Article 9 of this convention, which came into force in September 1953).

In 1981, the General Assembly of the United Nations adopted an even stronger resolution, calling for the removal of all expressions of intolerance and discrimination. There is a challenge to us in this context. In a concern to proclaim the unique gospel of Christ and expose error, we must at the same time support and safeguard the principle of religious freedom for all who live in our society, whatever their beliefs.

This is not compromise. And it is not a move towards a softer or inclusive attitude towards error. Not at all. But it is acknowledging people's right to have freedom of thought, conscience and religion in our democratic society.

Withdrawal

Another advantage from the sociological use of the term 'sect' is the understanding and perceptive insight which sociologists provide with regard to the emergence, nature and development of such groups in society.

I find this aspect of the subject fascinating and enlightening. For example, whether you use the term 'sect' or 'cult' or 'NRM', you are describing a minority that constitutes less than 1% of the UK population. For a variety of reasons, these people do not adhere to dominant forms of religion. Such individuals are usually different in what they believe and do. And they can be glaringly different from, for example, Roman Catholics or Protestant Christians.

Yet the differences are even more profound when viewed in the context of the secular society. A Jehovah's Witness, for example, is not allowed to attend school assemblies and RE lessons, join the Armed Forces, or participate in local or national politics. In spite of recent 'relaxations', they still cannot receive a life-saving blood transfusion without risking excommunication. The element of withdrawal from society can be prominent in some groups.

Protests

Sects, in varying degrees, are protest movements against Christendom and especially against a secularized society. Secularizing processes continued within society during the nineteenth and twentieth centuries and accelerated from the 1950s onwards.

In the past, churches fulfilled numerous vital functions for society. They provided social cohesion, a sense of identity, a theological framework for morality (with its restraints and rewards), and social concern and comfort for the suffering and dying. But secularization has profoundly affected the church, resulting in widespread fragmentation of religious and social values. Group identity now tends to be expressed more in terms of political, economic class or ethnic boundaries. It is no longer the church that provides support and counselling for the needy, but secular agencies and specialist professions.

Change

Profound and broad social changes, therefore, have occurred in British society over the past decades, and there are many causes and indicators. One indicator relates to family life. In England and Wales, church marriages have fallen from 251,368 in 1970 to 77,500 in 2000.

UK divorces have doubled since 1976 to 155,000 in 2000; 14% of men and women in England and Wales cohabit. The number of children under sixteen in England and Wales, whose parents are divorced, has soared from 82,304 in 1971 to 159,671 in 1996. Of these, 44% are aged between five and ten. Just over 40% of births were outside of marriage in 2002, more than four times the proportion seen twenty-five years earlier.[1]

Sociologists then can assist our understanding of these complex changes and explain the 'appeal' of new or older 'sects' or 'cults' in the context of these shifting moral and social sands.

Criticism

However, this use of the term 'sect' can be criticized in two ways. First, there are major differences between sects in the past and contemporary ones. Historically, sects were schisms within and from the dominant church. Today that is rarely true, for sects can be secular, Oriental or post-Christian, with no links at all with Christian churches.

Secondly, as Christians we must insist on a theological evaluation of what a sect teaches. There is no choice for us. Why not? Because the Bible is God's Word and his only Word. God is its author and the words as well as the teaching of the Bible are his in their entirety (2 Timothy 3:16; 2 Peter 1:21).

For that reason, the Bible is reliable in all that it says. All beliefs, experiences and practices, whether social or religious, must be tested by this sole authority. And that is why Christians, unlike sociologists, must and do evaluate sects from a Bible perspective.

There is a further and related reason. The Bible gives the only answer to human sin, guilt and estrangement from God. And that answer centres in the cross of Christ. God the Father punished his only Son in our place so that we can be right with God. The death of Christ for sinners is an astonishing demonstration of amazing love. All we must do in response is to 'believe in the Lord Jesus' (Acts 16:31). At the moment of trusting Christ, we are saved.

For these reasons, I prefer not to use the term 'sect'. What about the terms 'cult' and 'NRM'? These will be dealt with in the next chapter.

THE GUIDE

CHAPTER TWO

REFLECTIONS: THE TERMS 'CULT' AND 'NRM'

A BRIEF HISTORY

'Do you belong to that cult?' That was the question thrown at me unexpectedly as I visited some houses in north-west Wales. Before I could answer, the man continued, 'Do you belong to those who go around with a Bible, refusing blood transfusions for their children when they are dying?'

He thought I was a Jehovah's Witness. After explaining I was a Christian and the pastor of a church nearby, he became more relaxed. 'The only religious people who come round these houses', he added, 'are Mormons and JWs. I did not expect church people to call at my house.'

I felt his words were extremely challenging. For almost an hour we talked freely about the gospel as we drank tea together in his home.

Odd people?

But it is that word 'cult' again. For this man the word was associated with odd, unusual people who did 'strange', even 'extreme' things.

Now this is the word we are thinking about in this chapter, together with the term 'new religious movement' (abbreviated to NRM). There is need to reflect on their meaning and the use of such terms.

What do these words mean? The main problem, of course, is with the word 'cult'. And we need to unravel its meaning and find out how it is being used today.

Where do we start? Is the *Concise Oxford Dictionary* a useful starting point? Not really. A cult, it tells us, involves 'a devotion or homage to a person or thing'.[1] The word can also refer to 'a popular fashion especially followed by a specific section of society'.

Strong devotion to a leader and to an organization certainly characterizes a significant number of cults. But there are other features, too, which are equally important. So this definition is only partially helpful.

Embedded

The term 'cult' is ambiguous as well as complex. The term is elastic too, in the sense that it is often stretched to varying degrees depending on the commentator. Should we, then, abandon this word? I think not, and for four good reasons.

One reason is that the word has become embedded in modern jargon. All kinds of people use it. I taught an undergraduate degree module on NRMs. The students came from widely different social backgrounds but they all described it as 'the cults course'! So because the ordinary person on the street uses this word, it is part of modern parlance and we need to retain it.

Secondly, and related to the above point, the media consistently use the term 'cult'. The *Daily Mail*, for example, has campaigned successfully against the more sinister cults. On radio and TV it is this word 'cult' that is mostly used by interviewers and contributors to describe the phenomena we are discussing.

Government use

Thirdly, the term is used in government circles. One example in 2001 was the government's ban preventing religious organizations from holding television broadcast licences. Ministers were apparently open to suggestions on how the restrictions could be eased.

Government concerns related to increased choice in the digital future, the content and aims of religious broadcasting, and the danger that irresponsible groups might fuel racism. Organizations like the Universal Church of the Kingdom of God own about twenty television and fifty radio stations in Brazil.[2]

Speaking on behalf of the Cult Information Network, Ian Howarth said that he did not object to 'main-stream' churches starting digital TV stations but felt that cults should be banned.

'Cults, by definition, remove personal freedom,' he declared. 'The definitions in any new legislation would have to be very tight. It is interesting that in the UK we allow cults to register as charitable institutions in the same way as religious or therapeutic organizations.'

This matter of broadcasting licences needs to be monitored by Christians, but I am using the example here only to illustrate the point; the term 'cult' enters into government discussions and planning. MI5 also reported to the UK government in 1999-2000 concerning some cults.

Common features

Fourthly, while there are many differences among cults, there are features that apply to most, if not all, of them. These features include factors such as protest and withdrawal; a strong allegiance to leaders; and a degree of control over members that reduces (or even removes) personal freedom. When people use the term cult, they are usually referring to one or more of these features.

It is helpful, therefore, to retain the word 'cult'. Unlike the term 'sect', the word 'cult' has a wider, less Christian, base. Consequently, it is fairly comprehensive in covering the many groups exhibiting cultic tendencies that have emerged in recent decades.

What other features do cults have in common? As we saw in the last chapter, protest is a dominant feature, whether it is expressed against major religions, a state church and/or the secularizing of society.

The element of protest is often expressed by varying degrees of withdrawal from society. For example, the

Nameless Group, the Cooneyites and others endeavour to insulate and separate themselves from society in many basic ways. One such member related to me how his childhood was unhappy on account of the strict policy of isolation from society. He felt rejected and the long-term effects were low self-esteem, paranoia, depression, anxiety and guilt coupled with fear. The sense of isolation can be overwhelming.

Allegiance

Then there is the feature of strong allegiance to a leader and organization. Whether it is the Watchtower Society, the Branch Davidians, the Family of Love, the 'Church of Christ', Scientology or the Order of the Solar Temple, allegiance to leaders or an organization can be both blind and total. This has led many to conclude that cult leaders use techniques of mind control to exercise authority over members and develop in them a sense of dependence. In varying degrees, these features are found in the majority of cults.

I make a distinction between groups which are *cults* (that is, where all or most of these features are found to a significant degree) and those that are not cults yet exhibit some *cultic features*.

Even a Bible-believing church may develop cultic features such as a blind allegiance to a leader and restriction of the personal freedom of members. Sometimes a church can develop into a cult, as did the Family of Love and the 'Church of Christ'.

On the other hand, this can work in reverse when cults like Seventh-Day Adventists and the Worldwide Church of God attempt to reform themselves under the Word of God, ridding themselves of most, if not all, cultic features. The WCG is changing and is now a member of the Evangelical Alliance, subscribing fully to its doctrinal basis.

New religious movements

What about NRMs? This term is less offensive, offering more flexibility in describing the complex contemporary cult scene. However, many of the cults are not 'new'; and those that are 'new' are recycling old ideas.

The word 'movement' also is too grand to describe many groups like the Branch Davidians and the Family of Love. Furthermore, some cults, like Scientology, are not as 'religious' as they seem, so there are difficulties with the term NRM. One writer, David Barrett, favours using the term 'alternative religion',[3] because it avoids the problems of whether a group is a 'movement' and 'new'. But this term is unsatisfactory too. In Salt Lake City, for example, Mormonism is not an 'alternative' but a majority creed. Again, the assumption is made that all such movements are religious. For all the above reasons, the term cult, despite its weaknesses, needs to be retained and used in preference to terms like 'sect', 'NRM' or even 'alternative religion'.

Differences

There are, of course, differences between cults, which vary in the degree to which they practise protest, withdrawal, allegiance and control. Compare, for example, the Watchtower with Scientology. The former claims to be Bible based. It is Adventist in theology, zealous in proselytizing, and it protests strongly against Christendom, which it views as satanic and hypocritical.

Pressure is placed on members to engage in 'ministry', attend meetings and follow a specific lifestyle. By contrast, Scientology claims to be religious, although this is questioned by some. There have also been reports of financial exploitation and mind-control techniques being used on unsuspecting seekers which may not be true of the Watchtower.

In addition to the 'withdrawal-allegiance-control' syndrome, almost without exception a cult will display deviations from major Bible doctrines. This leads to a distortion of the gospel. That is the greatest tragedy, for the gospel of Christ alone tells sinners how they can be reconciled to the holy God.

At the heart of this gospel is the glorious news that Jesus Christ died bearing the punishment of sinners and rose again from the dead to declare them justified (Romans 4:25). To conceal, deny or even modify this God-given gospel is tragic, whether by cults or even mainline churches.

THE GUIDE

CHAPTER THREE

REFLECTIONS: SHARED FEATURES RELATING TO CULTS; TESTS

A BRIEF HISTORY

As we have seen, key terms like 'sect', 'cult' and 'new religious movement' are somewhat ambiguous and limited in their usefulness yet it is the term 'cult' that is more often used in modern parlance and by the media.

It will be no surprise to you that the term 'cult' has been in the news in recent years.

Cults in the news

An unusual story concerned the former Roman Catholic Archbishop of Lusaka, Emmanuel Milingo, who at the age of seventy-one flabbergasted the Vatican by marrying a member of the Moonies, a cult which is officially called the Unification Church.

Almost thirty years younger than himself, his bride was Maria Sung. Hours before the ceremony, a Vatican spokesman appealed to the archbishop not to proceed with the marriage; but the 'Moonie wedding' took place as scheduled. Sung and Milingo were one of sixty couples joined in wedlock by the Korean cult leader, Rev. Sun Myung Moon, in the ballroom of a prominent New York hotel. Milingo took his wife to Zambia in order to work among the poor and sick.

Polygamy

The Mormon cult has also been in the news. The reason? Utah State authorities have been embarrassed by polygamist Tom Green who has five wives and twenty-five children!

Green was charged with bigamy by State prosecutors. For Green, the charge was regarded as an attack on freedom of religion and expression. Many of his supporters felt that the legal action was motivated by the desire to remove all associations of polygamy from Utah and project a contemporary 'respectable' image before the Winter Olympics held in Salt Lake City in February 2002.

Polygamy has a long history in sections of Mormonism. But only nine years after President Lincoln signed the Anti-Bigamy law in 1862, the Mormon leader Brigham Young was arrested for 'lewd and lascivious cohabitation' with his sixteen wives! Polygamists are now, it is claimed, excommunicated by the cult.

What about American pastor Jack Stahl? Was he cultic? Has he created a cult? Or was he merely exploiting people? Based in Sacramento, California, Pastor Stahl was convinced that Tom Jones, the renowned 'pop' singer, is god. The claim is incredible and blasphemous. Belonging to the Progressive Universal Life Church (PULC), Stahl lists numerous spiritual blessings he receives in listening to the singer. 'I believe he is a god,' Stahl declares, 'and I worship him.'

The media is puzzled by Stahl, but also cautious. And the main reason for the caution is that Stahl's church 'seems just a little more financial than spiritual'.[1] Healing, ordination to the ministry (the cost is $150), 'doctorates' (a mere $170) and discounted air tickets, as well as hotel rooms, are some of the many things on offer from this man. Beware.

Shared features

The first point I am making by providing these examples is that cults continually make the headlines in news programmes, daily newspapers and news magazines. And the public is often intrigued, as well as disgusted, by what they hear about some of them.

My second point from the foregoing examples is that it can be difficult identifying some groups as cults. For that reason, in the last chapter I introduced the helpful distinction between a cult and a group/church or individual with cultic features or tendencies. For example, how do we describe Pastor Jack Stahl of California? Sociologists like J. Saliba identify negative features that belong to their recognition of a cult. Among these negative features are deceptive recruitment techniques, financial and psychological exploitation, the discouragement of rational thinking, total allegiance in terms of energy, time and finance, then the aura of mystery or secrecy. Clearly only some of these features apply to Stahl and that is why the media tend to suspect that he is using religion only as a lucrative means of making money.

Stahl's adoration of Tom Jones, however, is not only bizarre; it is total, cultic and idolatrous. For example, Stahl attributes his spiritual awakening, the effectiveness of his 'spiritual' work, the enjoyment of inner peace and the exorcism of evil spirits to Tom Jones. He also prays for his parishioners at his Tom Jones 'altar'. Stahl is in danger of developing his aims and ideas into a fully-fledged cult.

My third point is that while sociological and historical factors are extremely helpful in identifying, understanding and classifying cults, they are inadequate without the testing of claims, beliefs and actions by the supreme standard of the Bible. That must be the ultimate test, whether sociologists like it or not. I will illustrate this with regard to Pastor Stahl.

Biblical tests

'You shall have no other gods before me' (Exodus 20:3) is a divine command to which Stahl and everyone else should give heed. This allows no compromise at all. Positively, our duty is to love and obey the triune God with all our heart, all the time.

Negatively, God commands us not to give to any other person or thing the love and worship due to *him*. Furthermore, compared with humans who 'wither away like grass' (Psalm 102:11-12), the Lord alone 'endures for ever'; he remains 'the same' and his years 'will never end' (v. 27). For these reasons alone it is foolish to worship Tom Jones or any other human.

The Bible also provides us with another powerful but similar contrast. While people are like grass that withers, the Word of our God 'stands for ever' (Isaiah 40:6-8). And the apostle Peter in quoting these words adds: 'And this is the word that was preached to you' (1 Peter 1:25).

There is an enormous challenge here to us all. Fame, physical beauty and strength, wealth, even a good singing voice, will all fade away. Only God's Word is permanent.

But there is more to the challenge. God's Word is also reliable. It is completely trustworthy; God is faithful to his Word. And, thankfully, it is also a 'living' and powerful Word. As Alan Stibbs writes, 'God's Word never becomes obsolete or a dead letter. It continues to speak to people unchanging, vital, present truth. It continues to find completion and vindication in unfailing fulfilment.'[2]

And it is by means of this Word alone that people can be 'born again' (1 Peter 1:23), forgiven and reconciled to God in Christ. That is the gospel, and it is glorious news for people everywhere.

CHAPTER FOUR

REFLECTIONS: A CONTEMPORARY, WORLDWIDE PROBLEM

A BRIEF HISTORY

Cults are a contemporary problem. This point has already been illustrated and established in the last three chapters and also in Volume 1. In this chapter, our reflections will focus on the fact that cults constitute a worldwide problem.Consider this statistic, for example. Cults comprise at least 2.2% of the world's population. This percentage represents well over 100 million people.

China

Cults are certainly not confined to Western countries. The vast country of China, for example, has had problems with them in the past and this continues today. In more rural and remote areas of the country particularly, some cult members have been doing bizarre things like throwing themselves off a cliff or jumping into dangerous rivers in the expectation that they would be rescued supernaturally. Tragically, many of them died. Others have even killed their own children in a vain attempt to please God. These are only a few of the more extreme examples of cult activity in China but many cults are operating there.

South Korea

I was in the country of South Korea in October 1993. At times it was quite chilling because one cult had prophesied that the end of the world would occur on the 27 October. One problem I had was that my flight home was scheduled two days later on 29 October! In the newspapers and on the TV news we were being told of thousands of people who had resigned their jobs and sold their homes. People on the streets were talking about it. However, the cult members waited in vain for the end of world history. The police arrested some members, including the leader, for disturbing the peace and threatening national security.

In February 1994, a prominent Korean theologian, Tak Myung-Hwan, was murdered for speaking out against the cults. He was a godly, brave man who believed firmly in the Bible. He had received many death threats beforehand and had survived many attempts on his life, including a car bomb and a stabbing. The *Korea Herald* reported that members of the Daesong Church, an unorthodox and extreme organization, had claimed responsibility for the murder. It is estimated that about 350 cults in this country claim some Christian affiliation.

Japan

In Japan, cults and new religions have grown at a phenomenal rate and these have attracted mostly young people in their twenties. The world was shocked in March 1995 to hear of the activities of the Japanese religious cult, Aum Shinrikyo (Supreme Truth). This cult was linked with the sarin poison nerve gas attack on five Tokyo subway trains which killed ten people and left nearly six thousand ill, some in a critical condition. Japanese police later found stockpiles of lethal chemical compounds vital in the production of sarin in the cult's building.

Founded in 1987 by Shoko Asahara, this militant quasi-Buddhist cult taught that the end of the world would occur in 1997. It claims to lead people to mystical experiences through practices said to include swallowing water and vomiting it up in order to 'purify' their bodies.

This cult, renamed as Aleph, has acknowledged responsibility for the 1995 killings and the injuring of thousands. Ten years later in 2005, its leader is still before the courts in Japan. In February 2004 he was sentenced to death but lodged an appeal on health grounds. Towards the end of that year a Tokyo court ruled that Asahara was mentally fit and that the appeal would not be halted for any longer. The result of his appeal is expected during 2005.

Tibet

In another part of Asia, we have reports of the success of Scientology workers in Tibet. They have worked extremely hard over recent months and years to establish a base and gain recognition for their cult in the country. For example, one American Scientologist has spent a great deal of time there, especially in places like Mysore, Bylakuppe and Hunsur. Part of her work involved teaching Tibetan monks some of the techniques developed by L. Ron Hubbard, the founder of the Church of Scientology. She claims some success, and in late December 2004 reported that an elderly Buddhist monk in Hunsur had his high blood pressure reduced to a normal level after applying some of the cult's techniques!

In these various places in Tibet, the Scientology worker gave a series of lectures on human rights and on the cult's teaching. Sadly, hundreds of students in these centres also heard her speak and her influence has been considerable. Scientology has now become a member of the Indo-Tibetan Friendship Society which includes Hindus, Buddhists and people from other beliefs. On 19 December 2004 His Holiness, the Dalai Lama, acknowledged the contribution and work of Scientology.

Norway

Currently, Scientology is operating and practised in more than 125 countries. Their activities in Norway have been particularly notable in that the government of that country has spent large sums of money sending drug addicts to a controversial Danish treatment centre run and supported by Scientologists. The Narconon Centre in Denmark bases its treatment on the teaching of Ron Hubbard. There are now growing fears that Norwegian addicts end up as converts to Scientology after their stay. Ole Thiemer, the manager of the centre, acknowledges: 'We have clients that become Scientologists when they complete treatment. Maybe they think like I do, that if just a tiny part of Hubbard's technology can free them of addiction, what could all of his teaching do.'

Publicity

Celebrities certainly help to give worldwide publicity and prominence to some cults, especially in the west. One example is Orlando Bloom, star of *The Lord of the Rings* films, whose participation in a religious ceremony in England at the end of 2004 illustrates the teenager's wholehearted commitment to Soka Gakkai International (SGI). SGI is a controversial Buddhist cult which has a troubled history. Its leader, Daisaku Ikeda, is its absolute ruler. He is a business tycoon and the influential person behind a Japanese political party called New Komeito.

Ikeda has been described by some as 'a grasping power-monger'.[1] Music icon Tina Turner, and Patrick Duffy, star of the television soap opera *Dallas,* are other noted celebrity members of this cult. New Komeito and SGI are both feared by many people in Japan. One web site launched by former members aims 'to inform the world about the reality of Soka Gakkai, its anti-social activities and infringements on human rights, and to provide assistance to those who have suffered or are suffering from the distress associated with membership in Soka Gokkai'.

The Moonies

On 15 August 1999, BBC News reported that the Moonies cult was pouring millions of dollars into an area the size of England in the swamplands of Brazil's Pantanal region.[2] Many Brazilian politicians and church leaders are concerned about the Moonies' intention to create their own earthly paradise in the area. They plan to invest $2 billion in the area up to 2009, and build an airport. 2000 Moonies were already living on the site in 1999.

BBC News also reported on 14 October 2000 that the Moonies had acquired more than 300,000 hectares of land in the northern area of Alto, Paraguay. This purchase included the town of Puerto Casada where there are 6,000 inhabitants. The Moonies are thought to have paid $15 million for the land and they plan the economic reactivation of the area, including the export of timber and the construction of new river ports from which to transport their products to Asia. This cult already controls a newspaper in Paraguay, as well as buildings and yachts in Fuerte Olimpo, the area capital.

In the USA, the Moonies created and have sustained at vast expense *The Washington Times* which, they claim, has influenced American presidents, government departments and public opinion extensively over the past twenty-three years.

Africa

In Africa, as in South America, the situation is extremely complex but disturbing and urgent. Frequently over the past five years I have had requests for help from missionaries and national workers in various African countries who have been perturbed about cult activities in their areas. They had lots of questions to ask. For example, what do these cults teach? Are they dangerous? How should we deal with their challenge and presence in our area?

The situation is complex because there are thousands of African independent churches, some of which are extreme and wild in their claims and demands. In addition there are cults, either African or sometimes Western or Asian in origin, which exploit the situation in many countries.

'Doomsday massacre warnings "ignored".' That was the headline of an article in the *Daily Telegraph* on 31 March 2000. The article concerned the Ugandan cult, Movement for the

Restoration of the Ten Commandments of God, responsible for the killing of almost a thousand of its followers. Details of this cult tragedy are chilling and distressing. Possibly the total number of the dead will never be known.

In November 2004 in Benin it was reported by responsible national leaders that at least 115 students in various educational institutions in the country have lost their lives to violent cult-related activities over the past ten years. During the same period, 665 students were subject to strong disciplinary action by the authorities for their involvement in cult activities. Another 536 students were expelled by institutions and some 129 students suspended for varying lengths of time.

The West

We can now begin to come nearer to home and note some of the problems with cults in the West. The frightening Waco disaster in 1993 disturbed people in many countries, in addition to the United States where it occurred. We will look at this in more detail in the next section of the book.

In 1994 forty-eight cult members were found dead in two separate locations in Switzerland. They had been injected with a powerful drug before they died and plastic bags were tied round their necks. Many of them had also been shot. The victims were members of the Canadian-based Order of the Solar Temple. No wonder that a number of Western governments are now nervous about cult activity and new legislation is being considered to cope with the phenomenon.

The point has been made. Cults pose a challenge for churches. Some of these cults present a threat to individuals in society and even to national security. What I want you to appreciate, however, in this chapter is that cults are active in almost every country. The problem really is worldwide. And some cults like the Moonies, Scientology and the Mormons are rich and powerful. Here is an enormous challenge for prayer and evangelism — worldwide.

THE GUIDE

CHAPTER FIVE

REFLECTIONS: MI5 AND CULTS

A BRIEF HISTORY

Can you find a link between the following: MI5; police chiefs; senior government officials; the Millennium Dome; San Diego; a Tokyo underground station; and Armageddon?

You have probably guessed correctly. They are linked in various ways with cults. But what has MI5 got to do with cults? Evidently, MI5 was interested because of the possible threat from doomsday cults of mass suicides and organized violence at the dawn of the new millennium.

Overreacting?

Was MI5 overreacting? Surely an agency of such stature concerned with national security should simply ignore these bizarre groups? Yet experts in MI5's counter-terrorist section conducted a detailed 'threat assessment' of what they called 'apocalyptic and millennial groups'.

Their task was to explore the possibility that some group or groups might resort to violence by means of shootings, bombs or even chemical or biological attacks on the public. It was in this context that MI5 experts identified the 'apocalyptic and millennial groups' as posing the greatest threat to national security.

What evidence, if any, did MI5 have? Perhaps one ought to emphasize, first of all, that the MI5 chief approved the report from his counter-terrorist section. He used it as the basis for warnings to police chiefs and senior government officials concerning the threat of mass suicides and organized violence from doomsday cults operating in the United Kingdom and overseas. It is reasonable to assume, therefore, that the report was thorough and sufficiently conclusive to demand vigilance and preventative measures.

The evidence quoted in the MI5 report is cumulative and partly speculative. But it is rooted in a number of recent cult disasters occurring in countries across the world. For example, reference is made to the Japanese Aum Shinrikyo religious cult which launched a frightening nerve-gas attack on the Tokyo underground system in 1995.

The whole nation of Japan was startled by the methods used by the cult and also by their aims. Could a similar incident occur in London? It seems that it 'cannot be discounted'.[1] In fact, counter-terrorist officials in MI5 were fearful that some cults might try to poison reservoirs, carry out terrorist attacks on key installations or intervene in sporting or other national events.

This fear, of course, has been intensified since the terrorist attack on the World Trade Centre in New York on 9/11 (11 September 2001).

Mass suicide

There was also the possibility of mass suicides. The MI5 report refers to two cults in the West which initiated mass suicides. One cult was the Canadian-based Order of the Solar Temple led by Luc Jovret, who had recruited his members mostly from civil servants in Quebec. In two separate locations in Switzerland, forty-eight of their cult members were found dead. They had been injected with a powerful drug then shot; tied round their necks were plastic bags.

Another recent example of group suicide referred to by MI5 is the Heaven's Gate cult involving thirty-nine members. Their bodies were found in a rented mansion in an exclusive suburb twenty miles north of San Diego on 28 March 1997. The people called themselves angels and probably believed they were destined to rendezvous with a spacecraft travelling behind the Hale-Bopp comet when they agreed to their suicide pact. Applewhite, the cult leader, was regarded by his followers as an alien in human form!

Absurd? Yes, of course. But security officials could not rule out the possibility of this type of belief and action being popularized in the United Kingdom. In fact, the officials referred to a study by the FBI in America that concluded: 'Extremists from ideological perspectives attach significance to the arrival of the year 2000, and there are signs of preparations for violence.' Not surprisingly, MI5 felt the need to take action.

'Concerned Christians'

One other dangerous cult referred to in the MI5 report is Concerned Christians. It is an apocalyptic American cult but has dozens of members in Britain. The British leader is Tom Cook whose home is in North London. Cook actively distributes literature and propaganda videos for the cult but claims that they proclaim peace, not violence and war.

The leader of the cult is Monte Kim Miller. Born in 1954 in Colorado, USA, Miller began the cult early in the 1980s in order to challenge New Age influences and fight prejudice in the media against Christianity. While his intentions were good, he soon deviated from biblical teaching and practice, claiming to be the recipient of private messages from God. His prophecies increasingly were related to 'the end of the world in December 1999'. On 3 January 1999 the Israeli authorities arrested fourteen members of the cult on the grounds that the cult was intending to embark on violent action to instigate the Lord's personal return. These members were deported five days later to the United States.

ABC News reported that 'there is growing concern in Israel that the group, the Concerned Christians, is a forerunner of hundreds of fanatics who will be drawn to

Israel at the close of the millennium'. No wonder that MI5 identified this cult as posing a potential threat to security in Britain.

The *Denver Post* reported fears in England that Monte Kim Miller and his members were targeting the Millennium Dome in London. Whether this was only a rumour we do not know, but the newspaper reported confidently: 'Scotland Yard will launch a massive operation to protect the site from all cults and terrorists ... The operation will cost about $10 million.' We will return to this cult for a more detailed case study in chapters 7 and 8.

'The Family'

The British-based group The Family, which wants to prepare people for the end of the world in 2006, poses less of a threat to national security. As part of their preparation, members are said to be 'stockpiling food' and preparing to hide in caves in India before the cataclysmic event occurs.

Thankfully, the eve of the new millennium did not bring the cult violence and mass suicides that security services such as MI5 feared. There was certainly tension in some countries, including Israel where soldiers patrolled the outer cordon of the ancient city of Armageddon (Meggido). Security forces were on full alert but there were no major incidents.

In Britain, hundreds of thousands of revellers poured into Central London on the eve of the millennium. Just after midnight the biggest fireworks display in British history lit up the London skyline with thirty-nine tons of explosives. There were no mass suicides, no threats of violence, no major disasters and no millennium bug! However, we should be thankful that government agencies like MI5 monitored the situation so thoroughly in order to protect the public and maintain law and order.

Supporting the State

Reflecting on that situation, I turned to Romans 13:1-7 and reminded myself of our responsibilities as Christians to the State. Submission to the 'governing authorities' (v. 1) is necessary because they are divinely established. And those who rebel against the authorities 'will bring judgement on themselves' (v. 2). It is strong language.

Provided that civil government does not expect us to violate God's law, we are to support our earthly rulers actively and prayerfully. Three significant statements are made in verses 4 to 6.

Firstly, civil authorities have the task of promoting and rewarding what is good (v. 4). Secondly, they must restrain and punish those who do evil. These are primary responsibilities of the State, and Christians should be pro-active in supporting the State in the execution of these tasks, rather than being passive, critical spectators.

CHALLENGE

After all, the third significant statement here is that the authorities 'are God's ministers' or servants (v. 6). Police, magistrates, members of parliament, cabinet ministers, councillors and civil servants are all 'servants of God' with clearly defined, God-given responsibilities.

After reading Romans 13, I recalled an African student preaching from 1 Timothy 2:1-3 in one of our college morning services. It was a helpful message. 'Why don't you Western Christians pray for your secular rulers?' he asked. He then explained verses 1 and 2: 'I urge ... that requests, prayers, intercession and thanksgiving be made for everyone — for kings and all those in authority.' 'Yes,' the student insisted, 'Paul urges prayer for civil rulers, even for cruel Nero who was the Roman emperor at the time.' 'Look what we are to pray for,' he said excitedly, 'that we may live a quiet and peaceable life in all godliness and dignity.'

Yet we should not pray only for peace in society. My African student showed us from verses 3 and 4 that our prayers ultimately are for a vigorous, fruitful evangelism to develop within a stable, peaceful society. Here is a challenge for all Christians, wherever we live.

THE GUIDE

CHAPTER SIX

CHRIST'S DEATH AND CULTS

A BRIEF HISTORY

The death of the Lord Jesus Christ is at the heart of the Christian faith. Not only is it underlined as a historical fact but the Bible explains the significance, necessity and achievements of the cross for us in unambiguous language. We are not left to guess as to its purpose; rather, God has given us in the Bible a definitive and infallible answer as to why the Lord Jesus died.

Make no mistake about it. At the centre of Christianity stands the cross of Christ. Here is some evidence. The death of our Lord is mentioned directly in the New Testament as many as 175 times. But the indirect references to his death far exceed that amount so it has an exceptionally important place in the New Testament.

Consider, for example, the first four books of the Bible, namely, Matthew, Mark, Luke and John. At least one third of each of these four Gospels is devoted to the subject. Donald Guthrie is one of many biblical scholars who confirms this point: 'In all the accounts of the mission of Jesus the cross stands out as the most important feature, and its significance is carried over into the rest of the New Testament.'[1]

Guthrie is correct, for when we turn to the Acts of the Apostles, once again the Lord's death is given prominence. Wherever the apostle Paul went, for example, he preached Christ and his unique death. One such occasion is in chapter 17 verse 2 when he preached in Thessalonica: '...he reasoned with them from the Scriptures, explaining and proving that the Christ had to suffer and rise from the dead'.

Reflecting later on his preaching in Corinth, Paul could tell the church: 'For I resolved to know nothing while I was with you except Jesus Christ and him crucified' (1 Corinthians 2:2). This was at the heart of the apostolic message and gospel. Later, he leaves us in no doubt as to why Jesus died on the cross: 'Christ died for our sins according to the Scriptures' (15:3). Other New Testament writers give the same emphasis (see, for example, 1 Peter 1:18-19; 1 John 2:2).

To unbelievers, this biblical message and emphasis is generally unwelcome and offensive. In fact, 'the message of the cross is foolishness to those who are perishing...' (1 Corinthians 1:18). The demand of the Jews at the time was for 'miraculous signs' whereas the Greeks looked for 'wisdom', that is, clever, interesting human philosophies. The divine message of 'Christ crucified' was, therefore, 'a stumbling-block to Jews and foolishness to Gentiles' (vv. 22-23).

In this chapter I intend to illustrate that the situation is no different today, for people still do not like to hear of Christ's death for sinners. The illustration involves a small, representative sample of contemporary cults in which their erroneous views concerning Christ's death will be compared with the Bible's teaching on this crucial subject. The comparison will be made under three key headings, namely, the necessity, the nature and the victory of Christ's death.

The necessity of Christ's death

In order to avoid any possible misunderstanding, two preliminary but major points need to be emphasized early in this brief section.

The first point is that God is not obliged to save anyone. Or to put it another way, people have no inherent right or merit in themselves to be justified by God and given eternal life. Because of our sin, all that we deserve is death (Romans 6:23).

There is a second and related point, which is that God saves only because he freely and sovereignly loves us. That is the ultimate cause for Christ dying on the cross for our sins. 'For God so loved the world that he gave his one and only Son, that whoever believes in him shall not perish but have eternal life' (John 3:16). Except for his love, God would punish all of us.

The following comparison may now help to clarify further what the Bible teaches concerning the necessity of Christ's death.

RELEVANT COMPARISONS

Cults	The Bible
The only purpose in Christ's death was to express the Father's love (Christadelphians).	While Christ's death has its origin in, and expresses in a glorious way, the infinite free and sovereign love of God (John 3:16; Romans 5:8), it has also the divine purpose of redeeming sinners to God (1 John 4:10).
The cross was not necessary, for humans are essentially good and God is only an exalted man (Mormons).	1. All humans are sinful, guilty and condemned (Romans 3:10, 23; 5:12).
No reconciliation of any kind is necessary between God and humans. All that is needed is enlightenment and meditation (Transcendental Meditation).	2. Having loved us and chosen to save us as sinners, Christ's death became necessary. John Murray describes this as a 'consequent absolute necessity'.[2] He explains the term: 'The word "consequent" ... points to the fact that God's will or decree to save any is of free and sovereign grace. To save lost men was not of absolute necessity but of the sovereign good pleasure of God. 'The terms "absolute necessity", however, indicate that God, having elected some to everlasting life ... was under the necessity of accomplishing this purpose through the sacrifice

of his own Son, a necessity arising from the perfections of his own nature', that is, his holiness and justice.

Romans 3:26: '... he did it to demonstrate his justice ... so as to be just and the one who justifies those who have faith in Jesus'.

Luke 24:26: 'Did not the Christ have to suffer these things and then enter his glory?' See also Hebrews 2:17.

The nature of Christ's death

In this section we ask, why did Christ die? What is the significance of what he did?

Jesus Christ expressed goodness and love; he is an example to follow (Christian Science).

Jesus lived a perfect earthly life (The Nameless Group).

Jesus Christ was an example in many ways; for instance, he never sinned throughout his life, not even when maltreated by enemies (1 Peter 2:22-23) and he always pleased his Father (John 6:38; 8:29).

He also performed many miracles and helped people in innumerable ways (Luke 4:31-41).

But Jesus Christ is more than an example and an expression of divine love. He is the God-man and the Saviour of sinners.

People are saved by Jesus' life and obedience rather than by his death (The Nameless Group).

'Without the shedding of blood there is no forgiveness' (Hebrews 9:22).

It was on the cross the Lord Jesus completed his work and obedience: 'It is finished' (John 19:30; see also Philippians 2:8).

It is an 'unrighteous, immoral' idea that Jesus should be punished for others on the cross (Spiritism).

In the infinite love and wisdom of God, the penalty due to us for our sin was inflicted by God the Father on his eternal Son, our mediator.

Referring to God the Father, the apostle Paul declares: 'God made him [Jesus] who had no sin to be sin for us, so that in him we might become the righteousness of God' (2 Corinthians 5:21).

This was clearly prophesied hundreds of years beforehand: '...the LORD has laid on him the iniquity of us all ... it was the LORD's will to crush him and cause him to suffer...' (Isaiah 53:6, 10).

The cross deals only with the sins of Adam.

Here the Mormons and Jehovah's Witnesses agree. The former maintain that Jesus' death dealt only with Adam's sins and it has no power to

The Bible nowhere limits the purpose of Christ's death to that of atoning for Adam's sins. On the cross, Christ offered himself as a complete and once-for-all sacrifice for sin — past, present and future.

save us. JWs confirm that the cross purposed to deal with Adam's sin only, not our personal sins. Christ's death provided an exact payment for what Adam lost, that is, perfect human life in Eden.

This 'ransom sacrifice', as they call it, is not a completed work but only the basis from which we work to achieve our salvation.

It is only because Jesus paid the full penalty for all sin that we can say, 'there is now no condemnation for those who are in Christ Jesus...' (Romans 8:1).

Sin was dealt with finally and victoriously on the cross; God's wrath against sin was fully poured out on Christ on the cross.

'... he has appeared once for all at the end of the ages to do away with sin by the sacrifice of himself ... Christ was sacrificed once to take away the sins of many...' (Hebrews 9:26-28).

The victory of Christ's death

The Moonies hold that the death of Jesus Christ was an utter failure. For them, Jesus' mission was to take a bride in place of Eve, marry then bear perfect children. By this act, other 'perfect' families would have been established eventually and the world, in the end, 'perfected'.

Moonies insist that Jesus failed in this mission because he was crucified before marrying. God

The Lord's words from the cross, 'It is finished' (John 19:30), were words of triumph. Having obeyed the law of God perfectly in his life and then, on the cross, suffered the punishment due to us, Christ had there victoriously purchased our 'redemption through his blood, the forgiveness of sins...' (Ephesians 1:7).

He was also victorious over Satan in his life, death and resurrection:

then allowed Satan to 'invade' the physical body of Jesus and crucify him!

'The reason the Son of God appeared was to destroy the devil's work' (1 John 3:8).

'...now the prince of this world will be driven out' (John 12:31).

On these words D. A. Carson writes: 'Although the cross might seem like Satan's triumph, it is in fact his defeat. In one sense Satan was defeated by the out-breaking power of the kingdom of God even within the ministry of Jesus (Luke 10:18). But the fundamental smashing of his reign of tyranny takes place in the death/exaltation of Jesus... When Jesus was glorified, "lifted up" to heaven by means of the cross, enthroned, then too was Satan dethroned...'[3]

In his death, too, the Lord was victorious over death (Hebrews 2:14-15).

'When the Lord said, "I go to prepare a place for you" (John 14:1-2)... He meant that He was going to remove every obstacle that stood between us and heaven and being with God and enjoying His glorious presence. He cannot prepare a mansion for us in heaven without first of all destroying the works of the devil, destroying sin and its dominion, destroying death and the grave. In addition to satisfying God's justice and God's holy law and offering this propitiation that removed the wrath of God, He had to do all that before He could prepare a place for us in heaven and then come back and receive us to Himself, that where He is we may be also.'[4]

SECTION E:

CASE STUDIES AND ISSUES ARISING

THE GUIDE

CHAPTER SEVEN

MI5 AND 'CONCERNED CHRISTIANS' (1)

A BRIEF HISTORY

One of the cults investigated in 1999 and identified by MI5 as potentially dangerous was 'Concerned Christians' and we will now focus on its beliefs and practices as one of two case studies in this section of the book.

Subtle shift

A forty-six-year-old American, Monte Kim Miller, is the founder and leader of the cult. His parents were not churchgoers but, as a young man, Miller himself professed conversion. He claims to have worked with Campus Crusade for Christ (now called Agape in the UK) for a one-year period, before becoming a sales and marketing officer for Proctor and Gamble from 1976-80.

In the early 1980s, Miller was a young, energetic man actively involved in helping churches. He was orthodox and zealous. He was also concerned about the anti-Christian bias in the media as well as the influence and teaching of the New Age movement.

At that time, Miller appeared to be concerned for orthodox, biblical truth and often spoke in churches concerning, for example, New Age teaching and similar trends which were beginning to affect Christians. There were no obvious grounds for suspecting that he would become a cult leader. His credentials were good.

We need to pause and reflect on the change in Monte Kim Miller. What happened? Where did he go wrong? Are there principles which can help Christians in our confusing, contemporary situation to avoid the same errors?

There are, indeed, major principles and lessons we can learn from Miller's sad story. But before pinpointing them, notice that Miller's shift from biblical teaching was subtle and gradual rather than sudden and obvious. To be precise, the change took place over a period of about eight to ten years.

No guarantee

While one can detect early indications of imbalance in his beliefs and attitudes yet, for a significant period, he appeared indistinguishable from other Christians and church leaders in terms of orthodoxy and zeal.

Clearly this is disturbing, but it reminds us of the Lord's parable of the sower (Matthew 13:3-9, 18-23). Here Jesus warns that there are different responses to the Word, some of which are only superficial and temporary because there has been no inward change or new birth. I am not saying that Miller is unconverted, for only God knows that. I am saying, however, that a profession of faith provides no guarantee that a person is truly born again. After all, the Lord Jesus declared: 'by their fruit you will recognize them' (Matthew 7:20). False prophets can come 'in sheep's clothing, but inwardly they are ferocious wolves' (v. 15). We need, therefore, to be alert and discerning in this whole area.

There are several major principles which are pertinent to the case of Monte Kim Miller.

Supreme authority

The supreme authority of the Bible is where we must begin, for this doctrine must be observed and applied at all times. If we go wrong here, we will go wrong in many other places.

I need first to explain this crucial principle. The Bible is God's book; it is where God has revealed himself and his purposes. It is a remarkable book, for God caused it to be written by men, yet reliably and without error. As a result, it is, word by word, God-given. What the Bible says, God says.

This being so, it is our duty to believe and obey all its teaching. All human opinions, theories and practices must yield to, and be tested by, the authority of the Bible. How do we know what God is like? Only through the Bible. Is it possible to find out what his plans are? Yes, but only in the Bible. Can we know God and be right with him? Certainly, but again only through the Bible. Are there God-given standards and directions for daily living? There are, and they are in the Bible. And let me add that *all* this information is *only* in the Bible.

Applying this principle to Miller and the 'Concerned Christians' is interesting, but it is also alarming and challenging. There is no evidence that Miller undertook a formal Bible college course. In fact, he disliked relying on others for instruction or advice, aiming to be taught only by God.

Newsletters

The aim was good but subjectivism and arrogance began to creep in. Miller imagined he did not need instruction or correction, even from godly, well-taught Christians. By about 1985 he began to deviate from Bible doctrine. At the same time, Miller claims to have begun speaking with God. He is not simply referring to prayer at this point. Rather, he imagined he was conversing personally and directly with God.

The year 1988 marked another change in his development. By means of several newsletters, Miller rightly criticized the Roman Catholic Church and the Word-Faith Movement. The latter has a long and complex history, but can be traced back to the writings of E. W. Kenyon. This author, who was influenced by cults like Christian Science, was recycled by Kenneth Hagin, who came into prominence in the early 1970s with the founding of the Rhema Bible Training Centre in Oklahoma.

Well-known leaders of the Word-Faith Movement include Oral Roberts, Kenneth Copeland, Morris Cerullo, Benny Hinn and Rodney Howard-Browne. In addition to prosperity and 'positive confession' teaching, many in this movement teach that God's Son, Jesus Christ, died spiritually and needed to be reborn spiritually because he had become a lost sinner under the mastery of Satan.

That is gross error. Miller rightly tested such man-made theories by the supreme standard of the Bible, and found them to be unbiblical.

Ridiculous claims

However, after upholding the Bible in this way, Miller began to criticize Bible-believing Christians and denominations like the Southern Baptists, Pentecostals and Evangelicals, for their American patriotism.

In the early 1990s, Miller finally isolated himself from Christians and claimed to be receiving direct and regular messages from God. These messages were almost entirely prophetic and apocalyptic. He made ridiculous claims. For example, he claimed to be one of the two witnesses of Revelation 11 and that he would be killed in Jerusalem in December 1999, but resurrected three days later. He also predicted that an earthquake would destroy Denver, Colorado, on 10 October 1998 and that he is the 'end-time true prophet to the world'.[1]

At the final judgement, he taught, everyone in the world will be compelled to kneel before him! In the meantime, he instructed his followers not to support or be involved in political and secular government. Many other examples can be given of Miller's absurd, unbiblical claims and teachings.

Able to make us wise

His isolation from Christians was a significant factor in his move away from the Bible, especially as there are groups of people who believe everything he says. That is tragic. Even more tragic is Miller's teaching that forgiveness of sins and salvation are earned through him, that is, by repenting and following him.[2] Any refusal to do this, he threatens, will result in execution by God.

Such teaching is condemned by the Bible. Only God can forgive sins (Mark 2:7), and that forgiveness was obtained for us by Jesus Christ alone. It is Christ, not Monte Miller, who '[made] peace through his blood, shed on the cross...' (Colossians 1:20).

Submission to the supreme authority of the Bible is crucial, for only this God-given book is 'able to make you wise for salvation through faith Christ Jesus' (2 Timothy 3:15).

We will continue this case study in the next chapter.

THE GUIDE

CHAPTER EIGHT

'CONCERNED CHRISTIANS' (2)

A BRIEF HISTORY

As we saw in the last chapter, one of the cults MI5 identified in their report as being potentially dangerous was Concerned Christians. Having already described the cult's emergence, and their failure to submit their beliefs and practices to the supreme authority of the Bible, we will now underline two other principles with regard to this cult.

Sufficiency of the Bible

Related to the Bible's supreme authority is the crucial principle of the Bible's sufficiency. What does this mean? Basically, it tells us that all we need for knowing and pleasing God is found in the Bible.

If you want principles of guidance for your life or church, and want to understand what God plans to do in the future, then it is to the Bible you must turn. You do not need any other 'special' book, revelation or prophecy. The reason is obvious. Only in the Bible has God given us this special revelation of himself and his plans.

At this point the cults, like some religions, make a disastrous mistake which can be illustrated by reference to Concerned Christians. Their leader, Monte Kim Miller, believes he is a prophet — and a special one, too.

Miller has claimed that God was using him as a messenger to speak directly to his followers. For example, he predicted that a major earthquake would affect the city of Denver on 10 October 1998. The result? Over seventy cult members left the Denver area after selling their homes, furniture and cars. And, of course, the catastrophe did not occur!

But this was not the end of his prophecies. Miller then predicted that he himself would be killed in the streets of Jerusalem in December 1999, then be resurrected three days later, ushering in the end of the world. Although proved wrong again, many folk still believe what he says.

Test the spirits

There are two tests we should always apply in this kind of situation. The first is to apply criteria from the Bible. For example, the words of Deuteronomy 18:21-22: 'You may say to yourselves, "How can we know when a message has not been spoken by the LORD?" If what a prophet proclaims in the name of the LORD *does not take place* or come true, that is a message the LORD has not spoken...' [italics mine]. By this test, Miller is not just a crank; he is a false prophet.

The second test is related, but highlights the sufficiency of the Bible. We do not *need* Miller's prophecies about the end of the world. It is important to grasp the reason for this. It is because the Lord has revealed in the Bible all that it is necessary for us to know about the future and the end of the world. This information is extensive and reasonably detailed. The Bible really is sufficient for us. To underline Miller's error even further, remember that the Lord Jesus condemns date-fixing. 'No one knows about that day or hour,' he insists, 'not even the angels in heaven, nor the Son, but only the Father' (Matthew 24:36).

How does God speak?

But there is another way in which the sufficiency of Scripture is denied by this cult leader. This relates to his claim to receive direct revelations from God.

Miller actually tells followers that God is speaking through him. Rachel Powell observed how Miller's followers, like Dustin Blythe, 'just sincerely believe that it's the Lord speaking, and they don't want to disobey God — that's how seriously they take it'.

Then there is store owner Jack Hook, who became a close friend of Miller. The friendship ended in 1996, soon after he received a phone call from Miller in which the cult leader declared seriously and repeatedly: 'I'm speaking in the voice of God.'

Hook rightly dismissed this claim because he knew that God speaks now, as always, through the Bible. An Illinois housewife, Debbie, is representative of many of Miller's followers who heard his alleged 'God-speaking'. Her response was one of shock but also fascination, so she wrote down on paper some of Miller's pronouncements. It was almost three years before Debbie broke away from Miller and saw that he was contradicting the Bible and denying its sufficiency in claiming continuing revelation from God through his own lips.

No one needs additional revelation. Nor should you listen to individuals who claim private messages and revelations from God. Rather, we should rely exclusively on the Bible, for it alone is the authoritative and sufficient Word of God for all generations.

The end time

A final principle is that Christians need to be alert, and much less gullible, in recognizing cultic beliefs and practice. One indicator, as we have seen, is a group's preoccupation with the imminent end of the world. For those who do not know the Bible this can be scary, creating an unhealthy frenzy and fear.

A second indicator is the dominance of a single 'charismatic' leader who demands submission and obedience to himself and his interpretations, rather than to the Bible itself. Beware! This tendency is sometimes apparent in Evangelical circles.

Another indicator is the cult's claim to be the only group which possesses 'the truth'. This is usually backed up by the claim that the cult is to exercise a unique, major role in bringing about the end time.

Fourthly, the leader, or leaders, dominate and closely control members. There is clear evidence that Miller isolates his followers from their own families and controls their lives, even to the point of how they should spend an evening.

A fifth indicator is doctrinal: a cult modifies or denies major Bible teachings. Always test what people teach by the standard of Scripture.

One never knows

Do 'Concerned Christians' pose a threat to society? London academic Eileen Barker is unsure, but adds, 'One never knows.' The Religious Tolerance organization in the United States suggests that the cult is peaceful in intent. They point to the fact that security forces in Israel and the West 'have made public only accusations of violent plans'.

Beyond the security and sociological aspects of this debate, however, one needs to give priority to the biblical dimension. The Lord Jesus warned, 'Many false prophets will appear and deceive many people' (Matthew 24:11).

This is reinforced by the apostle Paul: 'The Spirit clearly says that in later times some will abandon the faith…' (1 Timothy 4:1). Church leaders, therefore, need to be vigilant in ensuring that all their teaching is thoroughly biblical.

But the best antidote to false religion is the gospel of God's grace in Christ. The 'glorious gospel of the blessed God' (1 Timothy 1:11) must be preached urgently, prayerfully and widely. This is the gospel of grace, centring in 'Christ Jesus [who] came into the world to save sinners' (v. 15). No one else can save.

In the next chapter, we begin a four-chapter case study of the Branch Davidians in Waco.

RELEVANT COMPARISONS

'Concerned Christians'	The Bible
BIBLE	
In addition to the Bible, God gives special, direct revelation to people like Monte Kim Miller.	God says only what the Bible says; no additional revelation is given by God to anyone. 'To the law and to the testimony: if they speak not according to this word, it is because there is no light in them' (Isaiah 8:20, AV). See also 2 Timothy 3:16-17.

PROPHET

Miller believes he is a special 'end-time prophet to the world', making true predictions. He predicted that he would be killed in Jerusalem in 1999 and be resurrected on the third day; then usher in the end of the world.

'You may say to yourselves, "How can we know when a message has not been spoken by the LORD?" If what a prophet proclaims in the name of the LORD does not take place or come true, that is a message the LORD has not spoken. That prophet has spoken presumptuously...' (Deuteronomy 18:21-22. See also Jeremiah 23:33-38; Matthew 24:11).

FORGIVENESS/SALVATION

Forgiveness and salvation are achieved through Miller and by following him and repenting.

'...Who can forgive sins but God alone?' (Mark 2:7).

'In him [Christ] we have redemption through his blood, the forgiveness of sins, in accordance with the riches of God's grace that he lavished on us...' (Ephesians 1:7-8).

FINAL JUDGEMENT

At the final judgement, everyone will be forced to kneel before Miller and honour him.

'...at the name of Jesus every knee should bow ... and every tongue confess that Jesus Christ is Lord...' (Philippians 2:10-11. See also 1 Corinthians 15:24-28).

THE GUIDE

CHAPTER NINE

WACO: BRANCH DAVIDIANS

A BRIEF HISTORY

It was 19 April 1993 and the first week of our college summer term. At the end of one class a little before 11.00am, I walked down the corridor towards my room only to be greeted with the news that there was an urgent telephone call waiting for me. Rather hurriedly I went to the telephone to learn that the producer of the BBC TV Welsh News was anxious to talk to me. Almost his first words were, 'Have you heard the latest news from the USA?' I had not heard the news report that morning so the producer provided me with an update. 'The Waco problem', he informed me, 'has ended as a major tragedy.' He was, of course, referring to the Branch Davidian cult headquarters in Waco in Texas.

For months the signs had been ominous and things were beginning to get out of control. Government authorities were anxious to intervene but there was uncertainty as to the most effective response. Earlier, on 28 February 1993, four United States FBI agents had been killed as authorities raided the cult headquarters. 'What has happened now?' I asked the BBC producer. 'Well,' he replied, 'United States agents launched an assault on the headquarters using tanks, tear-gas, rifles and machine guns.' To me it seemed as if government authorities had overreacted, although the cult members themselves were well equipped with guns and ammunition; they were more than prepared to defend themselves and, if necessary, kill the 'aggressors'. I was then told the distressing news: 'The Waco compound has been burned to the ground and at least eighty-five cult members died, including the leader. Others have also been injured.' It really was a tragedy and the event received worldwide media coverage. For several minutes I discussed the significance of the incident with the producer and agreed to be interviewed about it on the BBC evening news programme.

Waco has not been an isolated incident. On 18 November 1978 in the Guyana forests, 913 members of Rev. Jim Jones's 'People's Temple' cult committed suicide at the command of their leader. The members dutifully lined up to drink orange squash mixed with cyanide. As we have mentioned before, in two separate locations in Switzerland on 5 October 1994 forty-eight cult members of the Canadian-based Order of the Solar Temple were found dead. Many of them had been shot but all had been injected with a powerful drug beforehand and plastic bags tied round their necks.

The cult tragedy, however, extends beyond the Western hemisphere to all continents. For example, we have already referred to March 1995 when the Japanese religious cult, Aum Shinrikyo (Supreme Truth), was involved in the sarin poison nerve gas attack on five Tokyo subway trains. Ten people were killed but nearly 6,000 commuters inhaled the gas, some of whom were critically ill for days. On 6 October 1998, *The Times* newspaper reported that seven members of a South Korean cult burned themselves to death in a self-sacrifice ritual in a van in a remote area east of Seoul. Among the suicides was Woo Jong Min, fifty-three-year-old pastor of the Yongsaeng (Everlasting Life) Church. These tragedies are the tip of an iceberg and it is feared that in the future a sequence of similar, if not worse, tragedies will occur in different parts of the world.

While focusing on the Waco incident and background, I want, in this second case study, to discuss some questions and principles arising from Waco which have a wider significance for cults in general and also for the Christian church. However, in this chapter it is necessary to outline briefly the history of the Branch Davidian cult in order to provide the necessary background for our discussion.

History

The story begins with a man named Victor Houteff who was born in Bulgaria in 1885 but whose family later emigrated to the United States. As a young man Houteff joined the Seventh-Day Adventist Church (SDA) but gradually he began to disagree with some of the official Adventist teaching. Houteff endeavoured to reform the Adventist Church theologically but his views and efforts were not welcomed by its leaders. One area of disagreement was the crucial doctrine of justification by faith which Houteff rightly wanted to emphasize. He claimed Adventist support for his position by referring to two Adventists who in their 1888 General Conference insisted that justification was by faith in Christ alone. 1888 was in many ways a watershed in the history of Seventh-Day Adventism as the doctrine of justification was given more prominence in the movement. However, the controversy continued and the nature of justification as well as its relationship to sanctification were debated for decades. But even Houteff's view on justification by faith was far from clear and Adventism obscured this biblical doctrine.

Justification

By contrast, notice that the biblical teaching is clear and uncompromising. As sinners, we are all guilty and condemned by the holy God. Nevertheless, 'It is God', and God alone, 'who justifies' (Romans 8:33). The word 'justify' in the Bible means to declare sinners righteous in relation to God's law. And God does this justly but freely and mercifully on the basis of Christ's unique sacrifice for sinners on the cross. Not only did the Lord Jesus suffer the punishment due to his people because of their sin but his obedience and righteousness are actually credited or imputed to believers. This means that the person who trusts in the Lord Jesus is acquitted, freed from the sentence of condemnation and accepted by God without any contribution at all by us. That was the issue in Adventism concerning justification. 'To the man who does not work but trusts God who justifies the wicked, his faith is credited as righteousness' (Romans 4:5). Over the centuries this clear biblical teaching has often been modified and compromised with disastrous consequences by individuals, churches, movements and cults.

Excommunication

Despite his genuine concern to uphold this teaching, Houteff himself was not clear on what the Bible taught and he seems to have implied that Christians can contribute to justification in some way by keeping the law perfectly. But that was erroneous, undermining the biblical doctrine. There were other disagreements he had with his church so he was formally excommunicated by SDA in 1935.

Along with a small group of followers, Houteff moved to property near Waco. Initially they were known as The Shepherd's Rod but in 1942 adopted the name Davidian Seventh Day Adventist. Houteff died in 1955 and then his wife assumed leadership of the group but her prediction that Christ would return in April 1959 led to some unexpected results. For example, one of her late husband's followers, Benjamin

Roden, a Texas businessman, announced that he was not only a prophet but also the 'sign' predicted by Mrs Houteff. He then started and led a new group which he called the Branch Davidians, whereas Houteff's group disbanded in 1961 only to be reconstituted as the Davidian Seventh-Day Adventist Association. This latter group is located in Exeter, Missouri, and still maintains Houteff's protest against the traditional legalism of the SDA movement.

It is the breakaway group, Branch Davidians, that we are now discussing. The group's emphases were on the imminence of Christ's return, the observance of Old Testament Jewish feasts and, of course, the exclusive possession and interpretation of revelation. David Koresh (his real name was Vernon Howell) arrived on the scene in 1981. His background was SDA and he had been taught to memorize Scripture as a child. In fact, his knowledge of the Bible was impressive. But he was a loner and never knew his father until adult years.

Koresh left the SDA church as a teenager when his romance with a pastor's daughter ended. The originally nice, quiet person slowly changed into a proud and ruthless individual. He engaged in a leadership struggle within the cult which ended in the mid-eighties in a shooting incident. Koresh became the Branch Davidian group leader and in 1988 he visited Britain under his proper name and successfully recruited about twenty members from among Adventists. He travelled extensively and cult members believed he was the only one able to open the 'seven seals' in the book of Revelation which would then trigger off cataclysmic events resulting in the end of the world as well as the promotion of cult members to heaven. Koresh went so far as to make the blasphemous claim that he himself was the Son of God and misappropriated for himself titles which belong uniquely to Christ.

The Waco tragedies of February and April 1993 were due in large measure to the bizarre claims and behaviour of Koresh. Why refer to Waco here if Koresh was so obviously wrong and odd? Well, we can learn important lessons and principles from the Waco tragedies. And that will be the theme of the next three chapters.

THE GUIDE

CHAPTER TEN

WACO: THE CHALLENGE OF KORESH

A BRIEF HISTORY

I am grateful to readers who respond to what I write. The responses are always interesting and useful. Some provide valuable additional information and insights into a cult, while others are extremely critical of what I write. But each response is considered carefully.

Mishandled

One critic, for example, was 'sorry' that I 'wrote specifically about Waco'. The reason? 'Because the situation was entirely different' from what I had described. That is a big claim to make. My critic continues: 'I met an educated US lady a few months ago who said we should not judge the US by what happened in Waco and told me of other examples in the US where some petty official with some authority abuses his authority.' The letter continues: 'The FBI agents were not killed by Koresh and everyone was killed because that was what those who organised this atrocity intended…'

I have sympathy with some of these statements. Certainly, I am not judging the USA by

Waco for two reasons. The first reason is that the USA, as a secular state, encourages and seeks to safeguard religious freedom, so that Waco is untypical of what happens there. Another reason is that similar incidents occur in other countries and continents, even in Western Europe. The correspondent also rightly raises questions concerning FBI agents and the US government. To put it mildly, the Waco incident was mishandled by the authorities and could have been avoided or, at least, prevented from escalating into a major tragic incident. But more of that again.

In the context of identifying lessons which we can learn from Waco, I want to indicate two specific challenges concerning David Koresh, the Waco leader.

Christian background

The first feature and challenge that needs to be noted is Koresh's 'Christian' background. In fact, this is characteristic of the leaders and founders of several Western cults. For example, Charles Taze Russell (1852-1916), who founded the Watchtower Society, was brought up by God-fearing parents who were Calvinists and members of a Reformed Congregational church in Pittsburgh, Pennsylvania. Until the age of sixteen he respected and accepted the beliefs of his parents, even subscribing to the *Westminster Confession of Faith*.

Similarly, Mary Baker-Eddy (1821-1913), the founder of Christian Science, had the privilege of being taught the Bible by sincere Calvinistic parents who were active members of their local church. Like Russell, she reacted against the doctrines of grace in her teens.

Another example is William Miller (1782-1849), who was converted in 1816 before joining a Baptist church. His later date-fixing concerning the Lord's personal return in glory attracted many people to him. This was how the 'Millerite' and Seventh-Day Adventist movements were launched, even though Miller personally acknowledged his error. It was an Englishman, John Thomas (1805-1871), son of a London Congregational church minister, who established the Christadelphians. His own beliefs slowly became unorthodox and intolerant.

More recently the former Worldwide Church of God leader, Herbert Armstrong (1892-1986), worshipped in a Methodist church in his earlier years. But he drifted away, disillusioned by the inconsistencies of church members and the lack of quality teaching in the church.

A cult that has hit the headlines for the wrong reasons during the last fifteen years is the Children of God, now renamed the Family of Love. The founder was David Berg (1919-1994) who later changed his name to Moses David; Berg's father was an evangelist in the United States. Berg himself became pastor of an Alliance church, and then assisted a Pentecostal pastor, before going into coffee-bar youth evangelism. Slowly he compromised his orthodox beliefs but his 'Christian' background is impressive.

Challenge to parents

While David Koresh's background was not as privileged as that of Russell or Berg, nevertheless it was 'Christian'. Reared by his Adventist mother, Koresh was encouraged to attend church, read the Bible and pray. In 1979 he was baptized into the local Seventh-Day Adventist Church in Tyler, Texas. His Bible and an electric guitar were amongst his most treasured possessions, and he spent considerable time daily in prayer. Although Koresh was later disciplined by the church for creating dissension, his commitment to the Bible and prayer continued unabated.

This 'Christian' background for Koresh and other cult leaders is challenging in many ways. One challenge relates to Christian parents, that they should pray fervently that their children might experience genuine conversion and continue to walk with the Lord according to Scripture. While acknowledging divine sovereignty, and the fact that only the Lord can regenerate and save our children, we should remember that the sovereign God uses means in bringing sinners to himself. Such means of grace include the primacy of the Bible, prayer, godly example and teaching.

Here are major implications for Christians, including parents. What prominence, if any, is given to the Bible in our homes? Do we observe family worship? How vital and relevant is it? To what extent do we pray for our children's conversion and growth in grace? The examples of a Susannah Wesley, or the mother of Hudson Taylor, or the father of John Paton, rebuke the lax attitudes of many Christian parents today concerning the spiritual standing of their children.

There is the further problem of second-generation 'Christians', highlighted by the foregoing references to cult leaders. Are our children really saved? Where are the evidences of grace in their lives? Here, then, is the first major challenge arising from Koresh's 'Christian' background.

Continuing in the word

Related to this is also the challenge for genuine believers to persevere in grace and in the truth of Scripture. 'If you hold to my teaching,' declared the Lord Jesus, 'you are really my disciples' (John 8:31). Perseverance in sound doctrine and obedience are essential marks of a true Christian.

Here lies a challenge to churches, to be vigilant in maintaining and ensuring sound teaching. Koresh's local church disciplined him and did so in an attempt to protect their teaching. The two-fold challenge to churches in this respect is underlined by the apostle Paul. He warned that 'savage wolves' would enter the church from outside and inflict damage on the Christians. However, the second challenge is even more frightening: 'Even from your own number [that is, from among church leaders and members] men will arise and distort the truth in order to draw away disciples after them' (Acts 20:30). The word 'distort[ed]' is rendered 'perverse' in the AV and 'misleading' in the NKJV margin. All these terms are appropriate. This is happening in sections of the conventional Christian church today, as well as in the world of the cults.

Knowing the Bible

A second feature concerning Koresh is his knowledge and reading of the Bible. One correspondent makes this valid point: 'Apart from anything else Koresh must have been something extraordinary in so far as he knew the New Testament by heart!' And there is no doubt about it, Koresh read the Bible avidly and memorized large sections of it. When he first visited the Mount Carmel community in Waco, as early as 1981, the leaders were impressed by his extensive knowledge of the Scriptures.

For Koresh, however, there were pitfalls. He was attracted to the more obscure parts of Scripture. The last book in the Bible, Revelation, fascinated him while contemporary events and their prophetic significance had enormous appeal. An Adventist background led him and others to expect a living prophet to emerge.

Koresh claimed that he was that prophet and referred to private but 'divine' confirmations of the fact. Followers were persuaded of his credentials by his vast and profound knowledge of Scripture. The Waco leader insisted that he had been divinely sent to 'explain and to do the Scriptures'. In fact, he claimed to be able to 'open the seven seals' of the book of Revelation. An aura of infallibility was attached to his Bible expositions and interpretation of contemporary events.

I will return to this theme in the next chapter, but there are danger signals here for Christians. While the Bible itself is infallible, our own interpretation is notoriously fallible. Do we recognize this? Are we guilty of wrongly attaching cultic status to some of our pastors, Bible commentators or conference speakers? Let us beware!

THE GUIDE

CHAPTER ELEVEN

WACO: DANGER SIGNALS

A BRIEF HISTORY

After the first major Waco incident on 28 February 1993, in which eight people died, there was time for the media to investigate the Branch Davidian cult and to reflect on the crisis, before the even greater tragedy of 19 April 1993 occurred.

The Guardian was one of the London newspapers which monitored, and attempted to understand, the Waco situation just a week after the February incident. However, the verdict of their reporter was brief and to the point: 'In layman's terms, David Koresh, aged 33, is a nut.'[1] According to the *Concise Oxford Dictionary* the slang term 'nut' denotes 'a crazy or eccentric person' or 'an obsessive enthusiast or devotee'. *The Guardian* reporter appears to have understood Koresh as a 'crazy' and irresponsible person but hastens to add, 'He wasn't always that way, it seems.'

The reporter cited the evidence of a former 'wife' of Koresh, Robyn Bunds, who claims that Koresh 'slowly changed'. Bunds added, 'He was really nice. He was humble. Over the years, though, he lost a lot of those qualities.' Her belief was that he had 'become obnoxious, foul-mouthed, pushy, because of the power he has over these people'.

Charisma

One characteristic of all cult leaders is the way in which they come to exert and maintain 'power' over other people. While all power may corrupt, some cult leaders like Koresh have been ruthless in their quest for power. The 1987 leadership struggle for the Branch Davidian cult illustrates Koresh's aggression. That struggle ended in a shoot-out and Koresh was charged with attempted murder, although the charge was later dropped. But there are many other ambitious and ruthless individuals who wield total power over a group of people, without achieving notoriety like Koresh. We need, therefore, to probe the matter further by discussing the controversial concept of 'charisma'.

One popular view is that charisma refers to personal qualities which attract the attention and approval of other people. Does the person, for example, have a pleasing personality or the gift of oratory? Do they exhibit self-assurance and competence, inspiring others? Is there a suggestion that the person has some control over fate and the future? These and similar characteristics are often regarded as contributing to, or even constituting, charisma.

Koresh certainly had some of these personal qualities. A rather intense and gifted person, he was a dramatic actor and especially awe-inspiring when addressing his followers. He was capable of generating extreme excitement. But is this an adequate explanation of his appeal? I think not.

Relational

Another approach claims that charisma develops within a relationship between leaders and their followers. In other words, contextual factors significantly reinforce the leaders' personal qualities, and even give credence to their claims.

With regard to Koresh, his phenomenal knowledge and memorization of the Bible marked him out as an unusual and 'extra-ordinary' person. People were extremely impressed by this ability. Some went further and began to accept his exposition of the Bible, especially of obscure prophecies in the Old Testament and the book of Revelation. But notice some of the contextual factors operating to lend credence to Koresh's teaching.

Within an Adventist context, the end of the world was regarded as being imminent and a 'living prophet' was expected to reveal God's final message. A further factor in the background was the assumption by members concerning 'present truth' or 'new light'. This referred to 'truth' that they believe will be revealed progressively to

God's people as the world draws to its close. In practice, it was supposed to be new 'light' regarding the complete meaning of certain prophecies, and its significance for the remnant.

Attractive

Koresh's claim to have new understanding from God concerning the Bible was attractive to some people. For example, an Englishman with a master's degree in theology listened to Koresh speaking on the doctrines of God and salvation during his visit to Britain in 1988. The man, Livingstone Fagan, was impressed, and made several extended trips to Mount Carmel between 1988 and 1992.

What was the appeal? 'We were dealing', he explains, 'with an highly intelligent and systematic enquiry into the text of Scripture.' Fagan returned regularly to Waco 'in order to keep pace with the truths being revealed'.

Catherine Matteson, an older American woman who spent years in Waco, reports that those living in Mount Carmel were unwilling to 'miss something' that Koresh might be teaching. Members were eager to listen to his Bible studies. 'He gave prolonged Bible studies, yes,' she confirms. 'We might sit there for 15, 19 hours, 6 hours. It would depend. It was never a bore. He could have been a professional entertainer, the best this world has ever seen. He could entertain. He would have us in stitches. We'd sit there for hours. It was just great being around him.' These Bible studies were held each morning and evening, as well as a twice-daily breaking of bread.

Trapped

There was clearly a sense of excitement and anticipation within the Waco group. They imagined that the latest revelation or interpretation of biblical prophecy was being imparted divinely through David Koresh. Not only was there acceptance of Koresh's leadership and teaching, but there now developed a growing dependence on him, and admiration for him, on the part of community members.

In fact, many thought that their eternal destiny hinged on their fidelity to Koresh's teaching. They were trapped, especially in that he claimed to be the Lamb who opens the sealed book, referred to in Revelation chapter 5. According to Koresh, opening the seal meant that he himself had been given the unique task of seeing through the major cataclysmic events which would usher in the end of the world. His followers, therefore, believed he was a 'Christ' figure, although not to be identified with the historical Christ. Even the name Koresh, which he adopted later, was pregnant with meaning, for it was the Hebrew name for Cyrus referred to in Isaiah 45:1.

Danger signals

The danger signals here for Christians are clear. An eloquent, entertaining and dramatic speaker may be wrong when explaining the Bible. Sadly, error can be recycled in attractive forms. Remember, too, that no human person can provide an infallible exposition of the Bible. This does not mean we should disparage reliable preachers of the Word. In fact, we are exhorted to 'hold them in the highest regard in love' (1 Thessalonians 5:13) and give them 'double honour' (1 Timothy 5:17). But we must not idolize them nor regard them as infallible messengers.

Challenge

In conclusion I want to underline a three-fold challenge to readers. First of all, read your Bible often and extensively. After all, it is the Word of God. Enjoy reading, then applying its teaching to your life.

Secondly, identify sound principles for interpreting the Bible. That is where Koresh and many others have gone wrong. Such principles include interpreting Scripture by Scripture; bearing in mind its original meaning and purpose; placing a text in its context; and relying on the Holy Spirit for understanding.

Thirdly, remember that the Bible centres in Christ. Any teaching that diverts attention from him is bound to be false. This Christocentric focus is invariably compromised by cult leaders, and Koresh's interpretation of Revelation 5 is but one example. According to Koresh, he himself is the Lamb referred to here; it is Koresh, not Christ, he insists, who will fulfil the prophecies. But the context clearly refers to Jesus Christ. The sealed scroll in verses 1-7 represents God's eternal purposes throughout history, and no one except Christ is worthy to bring these purposes to consummation. In verse 5 'the Lion of the tribe of Judah' implies Christ's incarnation, while the title 'Root of David' points to Christ as pre-existent Lord.

Christ the Lamb

The glorified Christ is frequently referred to as the Lamb in the Bible. He is the Passover lamb (1 Corinthians 5:7; Isaiah 53:6ff), 'the Lamb of God, who takes away the sin of the world' (John 1:29). Revelation 5:6 refers to the Lamb 'slain', referring to his unique death on Calvary where he bore the punishment of his people's sins. But the Lamb also 'stood', underlining the fact that Christ is risen and glorified (see Revelation 1:18). In addition, the Lamb is omnipotent ('seven horns'), omniscient ('seven eyes') and equipped with the Holy Spirit ('the seven Spirits of God'). When the Lamb (v. 7) takes the scroll out of the hand of the one seated on the throne, it refers to our mediator's ascension to heaven. There, he began to exercise his mediatorial authority, to govern the church and world according to God's eternal decree.

The point must be emphasized. Christ, not Koresh, is the Lamb referred to in Revelation 5. And it is Christ, and Christ alone, who saves sinners. Is he your Saviour and Lord?

THE GUIDE

CHAPTER TWELVE

WACO: WACO AND RELIGIOUS LIBERTY

A BRIEF HISTORY

Two days after the Waco holocaust on 19 April 1993, a newspaper interviewed Graham Baldwin, a former London University chaplain, who had previously helped to bring approximately 200 people out of various cults. With an eye partly on Waco, Baldwin remarked, 'It is no good people saying that everybody has a right to join any religion they like. I agree with that entirely, but people who join a cult do not know what they are getting into. They do not know that their freedom will be taken away.'[1]

Key concept

Freedom is a key concept in the contemporary cults debate, and this is the subject of this chapter. Related to freedom are the claims of brainwashing or mind-control techniques with regard to cults like Scientology, the Unification Church ('Moonies') or the International Church of Christ. But we can come closer to home. A growing number of Exclusive Brethren ex-members complain that they were prevented from talking to close relatives and friends. They were then banned from attending meetings if they did not respond positively to their leaders' rigid directions concerning their lives.

For example, members of this group are not allowed to mix freely with other Christians or work or study with non-Christians. Nor are they supposed to own 'worldly' things; a TV, a sports car and a speedboat are just a few of the many forbidden items! One ex-member reports: 'We are concerned that there is a controlling elite within the Brethren who have tremendous power over people's lives. The way they break up families and friendships is very cruel.'[2]

Response

A natural response is that of anger and protest, with a demand for restrictions (or even a total ban) to be placed on the activities of groups which threaten personal liberty. That was how many responded to the Waco incident. 'Why didn't someone stop that lunatic sooner?' was their cry. Some governments have intervened on occasions to restrict or ban specific cults. In the mid-1980s the UK government imposed a brief ban on all overseas members of Scientology seeking to work at centres in Britain.

The question of restricting or prohibiting cult activities is a complex one. In the USA, for example, the First Amendment to the Constitution states: 'Congress shall make no law respecting an establishment of religion, or prohibiting the free exercise thereof...'

Freedom of belief is guaranteed to all, no matter how crazy their religious beliefs may be.

Article 9 of The European Convention on Human Rights (1953) is emphatic: 'Everyone has the right to freedom of thought, conscience and religion ... including freedom to change his religion or belief, and freedom, either alone or in community with others, and in public or private, to manifest his religion or belief, in worship, teaching, practice and observance.' It could not be clearer.

The United Nations Resolution of 1981 is even more extensive, for it eliminates all intolerance and discrimination based on religion. This resolution eloquently upholds the equality of all people before the law and their right to freedom of thought, conscience, religion, belief and the right of assembly together with their charitable institutions and teaching. Sadly, in many countries the UN Resolution is not applied for a variety of reasons. And only in recent years have countries like Italy, Spain, Portugal and Greece given concessions and legal rights to evangelical Christians as well as to cults.

Unacceptable practices

But, if we honour the principle of religious liberty, is it possible to prohibit religious *practices* which are deemed unacceptable? It is possible, especially if those practices distress or threaten other citizens and tend to undermine the State. For example, Christian Science has come under scrutiny for discouraging members and their children from seeking medical treatment, while the 'Family of Love' was investigated for encouraging sex between adults and children. In October 1994 the British Injuries Compensation Board awarded £5,000 to a teenage girl who had been abused from the age of three by members of this cult.

Other unacceptable practices include the financial exploitation of innocent victims by cults like Scientology, and the prohibition of blood transfusions by the Watchtower Society, a prohibition which can endanger the lives of Jehovah's Witnesses.

Tolerance

If specific cultic practices are prohibited, freedom of thought and religious belief should still be upheld. This means an attitude of tolerance in the sense of leaving people free to believe what they want. Democratic and secular states like the United States and Japan provide the greatest degree of tolerance, while liberal, democratic countries like Britain, France and Sweden are only slightly less tolerant.

Stunned by news that forty-eight cult members of the Order of the Solar Temple had been found dead in Switzerland in October 1994, some continental governments have been reviewing their legislation concerning minority religious groups. This review inevitably affects Protestant evangelical groups as well as cults.

A new law in Austria, for example, became effective early in 1998 requiring that any group seeking state registration should have 16,000 members, instead of the previous figure of 400. Some Swiss cantons have discussed measures for limiting the public activities of cults and the restriction of the use of the term 'church' only to denominations and groups approved by their police and justice departments.

This raises serious questions. Our forefathers struggled over a long period in the West, especially in seventeenth-century Britain, to establish the right to religious freedom for all citizens. We must pray as well as work to protect this principle of religious freedom. Civil leaders do need our prayers and it is our duty to pray for them (1 Timothy 2:1-5).

This need for prayer is also seen in the context of the Waco incident. The situation could have been handled better, possibly avoiding such a tragic ending. None of the FBI agents or Justice Department officials attempted to understand Koresh's mind-set or to listen seriously to his 'preaching'. A sense of deep frustration developed and an abrupt policy change was introduced when the FBI began its 'stress escalation' and harassment techniques which only further alienated Koresh and his community. These details are well documented and make sad reading.

Brainwashing

What about the controversial charge of brainwashing with regard to cults? Are techniques of mind control used to destroy critical ability among devotees?

Professor Margaret Singer, a distinguished clinical psychologist, gave evidence for the *Daily Mail* in the 'Moonie' libel trial in 1981. Objecting to an article in the newspaper in 1978 accusing them of brainwashing converts and breaking up families, the Unification Church lost the case and had to pay almost £1 million costs.

Allegations made by the newspaper against the 'Moonies' included the use of mind-control techniques, the recruits had a vacant look and were channelled into fund-raising work, and their motivation was strong; deception was also alleged to have been used to raise monies. These allegations are listed in more detail on page 188.

On the other hand, with regard to Waco we have reason to believe that all the followers of Koresh on campus were there voluntarily; they submitted themselves freely, and without coercion, to the teaching and directions of their leader. If it was brain-washing then it was subtle and effective but freely welcomed by members.

Drop-out rate

With regard to cults in general, Professor Singer argued that, on leaving the cult, most ex-cult members struggle with problems such as depression, meaninglessness, loneliness, indecisiveness, uncritical passivity and a deep fear of judgement, even recriminations. On the other hand, we must acknowledge that there is a large drop-out rate from the cults although some members claim to have found stimulation, purpose and fulfilment in a particular cult.

Furthermore, in their search for a 'faith', many individuals try different options until they find one they like. Interestingly, some cult workers are cautioned at times by leaders for being overzealous in pressurizing or brainwashing individuals. Authoritarianism, financial and emotional exploitation, then deception, are the more common criticisms made by new members inside a cult.

Greatest need

The dangers are real and some people suffer extensively through cult involvement. A tension exists between upholding religious freedom and protecting society from exploitation and deception. There is a constant need for vigilance and prayer. But there is a further challenge. The greatest need of people is for freedom, but the freedom they should be seeking is from eternal punishment for their sins and the tyranny of sin in their lives. And only in Jesus Christ can that need be met. He, and he alone, died as a substitute to free sinners from hell and reconcile them to God. 'So if the Son sets you free, you will be free indeed' (John 8:36).

RELEVANT COMPARISONS

Branch Davidians	The Bible
This group claims to have an orthodox view of the Bible, the Holy Trinity, the person and unique sacrificial death of Jesus Christ for sin, the physical resurrection of Jesus from the dead and his exaltation to heaven. The personal imminent return of the Lord Jesus in glory is also emphasized by them as well as the need for personal trust in Christ for salvation.	
Koresh's excesses centred mainly around himself and his claim to be the only one who could interpret the Bible accurately and also usher in the end times.	

Notice particularly four main errors with regard to his view of the Bible:

1. Koresh was the authoritative, unique interpreter of the Bible. No one understood the Bible like him.

1. '...their teachings are but rules taught by men' (Mark 7:7). See also 2 Peter 1:20-21; 2 Timothy 3:16-17.

2. A distinction is made between 'present truth' (that which is revealed in the Bible) and 'new light'; the latter refers to additional truth and details of exposition of the Bible which can be progressively revealed to a person as the world comes to an end.

2. The Holy Spirit alone gives understanding of his Word; this is given to all believers (1 Corinthians 2:10, 12, 13, 16).

No new revelation is given or added to the Bible by God. 'I warn everyone who hears the words of the prophecy of this book: If anyone adds anything to them ... And if anyone takes words away ... God will take away from him his share in the tree of life' (Revelation 22:18-19).

3. Koresh was the 'living prophet' to emerge before the end of the world and who received private, 'divine' communications.

3. Apostles and prophets were confined to the New Testament age; the church is now 'built on the foundation of the apostles and prophets, with Christ Jesus himself as the chief cornerstone' (Ephesians 2:20). No new prophet is needed for God

has revealed all we need to know in the Bible.

4. Koresh claimed he himself was the 'Lamb' in Revelation 5:5-8 who could 'open the seven seals' and be responsible for ushering in the end of the world.

4. The context in Revelation 5 is Jesus Christ. In verses 1-7 the sealed scroll includes God's eternal purposes in history. Only Christ, the mediator, has the authority and power to bring these divine purposes to fulfilment.

The title 'Lion of the tribe of Judah' in verse 5 suggests Christ's incarnation while the title 'Root of David' points to Christ as the pre-existent Lord.

THE GUIDE

Section F:

Established cults

CHAPTER THIRTEEN

MORMONS

A BRIEF HISTORY

The facts are staggering and we need to be aware of them. I am referring to the Mormons or, officially, the Church of Jesus Christ of Latter-Day Saints.

Did you know, for example, that there are now over eleven million Mormons worldwide? Each year they win more than 310,000 converts. What is disturbing is that eighty per cent of these converts come from Protestant church backgrounds. I will refer to this later, but in the USA Mormons often say among themselves: 'We baptise a Baptist church every week'!

Disturbing facts

Mormonism has the potential to exceed 267 million members within the next eighty years and thus become the first world-religion to emerge since Islam. Whether or not this potential will be realized, of course, is debatable.

However, there are other disturbing facts. The numbers of Mormon missionaries and converts will double in the next fifteen years. Already they are by far the largest single missionary-sending group in the world with more than 60,000 full-time missionaries.

These statistics are taken from a book edited by F. J. Beckwith, C. Mosser, Paul Owen *et al.* It is called *The New Mormon Challenge: Responding to the latest defenses of a fast-growing movement.*[1] The book is not easy to read but there are several reasons why, in my opinion, some church leaders should read it.

Apologetics

One reason is that LDS (abbreviation for the Church of Jesus Christ of Latter-Day Saints) has made huge advances in recent years in making its teachings appear more respectable to academics. LDS has engaged in a vigorous apologetics mission to commend its beliefs in a twenty-first-century context. The result is that there are Mormon scholars available today who are able to 'outclass many of their opponents' (inside cover blurb). Traditional arguments against Mormonism are now rejected as 'outdated, misinformed or poorly argued'.

If Mormon missionaries are active in our localities, are we sufficiently informed to engage with them biblically and in a meaningful way?

Well researched

Another reason is that the book represents the first major response by competent Christian scholars to the new challenge of more scholarly Mormon apologetics.

The contents are new and, in some respects, pioneering. There is no recycling of old material; the chapters are thoroughly researched — they are interactive yet do not compromise the unique, revealed gospel of our Lord Jesus Christ.

Challenges

Before discussing historical and theological developments within LDS, I want to indicate some of the contemporary challenges which this movement presents to evangelicalism.

One obvious challenge is a moral one. The LDS emphasis on the family unit, good family relationships, high moral values and consistency of behaviour often attracts new converts. Those who turn to Mormonism from Protestant and Catholic churches are often appalled at the inconsistent, often wicked, conduct of their previous church leaders and members.

Carl Mosser points to another challenge. He is convinced that 'a major factor contributing to Mormon growth is the widespread biblical and theological illiteracy among the laity of Protestant and Catholic churches' (p.69). His appeal is that our church members need to be 'grounded better in basic biblical doctrine'. This is not a call for all Christians to become professional theologians, but to be familiar at least with basic Bible teachings.

Christian basics

Are we failing here? Allow me a personal reference at this point. About four years ago I wrote an easy-to-read outline of major Bible doctrines. The outline, consisting of ten brief lessons and attractively packaged, forms a unit in my college's Correspondence Course.

I called the unit *Christian Basics* because the ten lessons are foundational, requiring and encouraging Christians to interact with the biblical text. My purpose in writing was to help new converts and others interested in the Christian faith.

Over the past four years, this 'unit' has proved extremely popular. To my surprise, however, many Christians of long standing have also opted to study *Christian Basics* and have felt comfortable with it. In fact, they benefited greatly from the studies and were encouraged to become more biblically literate.

This experience raises lots of pastoral questions in my mind. Do preachers and church leaders *assume* that their congregations know the Bible and its doctrines — when in fact they do not have a clear grasp of these things?

Again, are preachers communicating the truth at a level and in a way which believers can absorb and enjoy, becoming established in the faith?

Where do they come from?

Another challenge concerns the converts to LDS. Where do the 310,000 or more converts come from each year — in terms of background? One sociologist, Rodney Stork of Washington University, has researched this movement extensively over a couple of decades.

Stork has established that most of the Mormon growth is from converts rather than the children of Mormon families, with a ratio of over four converts for each child baptized. 'At any given moment', Stork claims, 'the majority of Latter-Day Saints are first-generation converts' (p.62). Where do they come from? Fairly reliable estimates indicate that 75-80% of them 'come from specifically Protestant backgrounds' (p.67). Mosser affirms that 'far more people convert to Mormonism from Evangelical churches than *vice versa*'.

This is a disturbing statistic, which is related to the lack of biblical literacy in churches in many countries, as well as to superficial forms of evangelism. An increasing number of Mormon converts are also coming from a Roman Catholic background; in fact, this trend is 'rapidly growing'.

Shock

There is a further challenge that may come as an even greater shock. The ability of Mormonism to extend its work into new cultures is 'literally dependent on the success of Bible translation organisations like SIL/Wycliffe Bible Translators' (p.68).

Three related aspects can be identified with regard to this challenge.

1. While LDS translate their *Book of Mormon* into many languages, they do not appear to engage in Bible translation work.
2. LDS missionaries are only sent to countries where the Bible has already been translated.
3. It is only against the background and knowledge of the Bible that the Mormon message makes its subtle but misleading appeal. Their message is that Mormonism provides the restoration of the 'fullness of the gospel'.

Mosser is correct when he observes that 'Mormon missionaries don't evangelize, they proselytize. Mormonism is a religion that gets its life mostly from pre-existing forms of Christianity' (p.68).

I wonder to what extent missionary organizations, including SIL/Wycliffe, are aware of Mormon exploitation of their work? Are there measures which can be taken to blunt this Mormon strategy?

Expository and doctrinal preaching

Mosser suggests that missiologists and missionaries need to 'develop strategies for effectively meeting the challenge' (p.83). He makes three recommendations.

First of all, because Mormonism is growing both on the mission field and in the missionary-sending nations, Mosser recommends more co-operation and consultation between pastors, church groupings, missionary statesmen and Bible college teachers in order to face this challenge.

Secondly, he recommends we develop apologetic and theological engagement and stop nurturing 'a cultural Christianity' or one so 'seeker sensitive' it can only be described as 'entertainment driven' (p.84).

Related to this, thirdly, he recommends a 'renewed emphasis on expository and doctrinal preaching in our churches', and the use of catechism as part of a more vigorously biblical ministry. I agree wholeheartedly with these recommendations. We now turn to look in more detail at Mormonism, its history, growth and teaching.

The work of Mormon missionaries is supported by extensive and attractive literature. In key areas expensive and elaborate temples are built as centres of recreation, culture and religion. The Mormon church takes tithing seriously, provides for its poorer members, thus rendering unemployment or social security payments by the government unnecessary, and encourages a responsible involvement in education, family and community life.

Their headquarters are in the state of Utah in the United States. It was Brigham Young, successor to their founder, who supervised the famous trek of Mormons to Utah in 1847, where they built Salt Lake City. They were not allowed recognition as a state within the U.S.A. until 1896 when they somewhat grudgingly agreed to ban polygamy among their members.

How it all began

The movement originally began with Joseph Smith (1805-1844) who, like other cult leaders, was psychic and the recipient of private 'revelations'. As a child he was confused by the numerous versions of the Christian church to be found in his home area of Sharon, Vermont. Although Wesleyan Methodism was the denomination he considered joining, he received a vision in 1820 in which, he claims, God the Father and the Son appeared, forbidding him to join any Christian denomination. The reason given to him was God's displeasure with their beliefs. As a result of the vision the teenager felt God called him to be his special prophet to the world.

Three years later he claimed an even more impressive vision in which he said an angel named Moroni disclosed to him the fact that details of the early history of America and a fuller revelation of the gospel had been written down in ancient Egyptian hieroglyphics on gold plates and hidden under the hill Cumorah. Although he wanted to see these plates immediately, he was told in another alleged appearance by Moroni that he would have to wait four years before retrieving them. Exactly four years later he returned to the place, obtained the plates and 'spectacles', or rather two crystals, by means of which he says he was able to translate the ancient hieroglyphics.

Scholars deny the existence of this ancient language and the supposed translation includes several errors in historical detail. The whole story was a great fraud. Conveniently for the Mormons, the alleged gold plates disappeared and before the publication of the translation, called *The Book of Mormon*, Smith and another five friends had established the Church of Jesus Christ of Latter-Day Saints at Fayette in New York State.

Growth and dispersion

Although this movement grew, it was also exposed to considerable ridicule and persecution, and Smith was compelled to move to a number of different places, including Kirland in Ohio, Missouri, and then Illinois, where in 1844 he was shot dead after being arrested and imprisoned for alleged immorality and dishonesty. Smith left the handsome sum of £400,000 and eight of his seventeen wives had died before him. He had as many as fifty-six children. Almost overnight he became a hero and under his successor, Brigham Young, who had even more wives than Smith (twenty-five, to be precise!) the movement flourished. Young eventually took the Mormons to Utah, arriving there in 1847, but not all of Smith's followers were happy with Brigham Young's credentials. One group, the 'Josephites', insisted that Smith's successor should be his son, so they withdrew, renaming themselves the Reorganized Church of Jesus Christ of Latter-Day Saints, and established their headquarters in Missouri. At least five groups splintered off from the main stream of Mormons, and most of them are still active today. The most powerful, however, is the party of those who followed Young, and it is their teaching that we shall consider.

The Book of Mormon

Early in October 1982, the First Presidency of the Mormon Church (its highest governing body, with a council of twelve apostles) unanimously voted to rename their *Book of Mormon* as the *Book of Mormon: Another Testament of Jesus Christ*. A spokesman explained the reason for the expanded title: 'We simply want to educate those who think the Mormon church is not Christian, to clarify that Jesus is a central figure in the *Book of Mormon*.'

Although the Mormon church was founded on the basis of the *Book of Mormon*, there exists a wide discrepancy between the book's teaching and that of contemporary Mormons. Three examples can be given to verify this fact.

First of all, the *Book of Mormon* teaches that there is only one God and he is an unchangeable spirit (Alma 11:26-31; II Nephi 31:21; Mormon 9:9-11, 19; Moroni 7:22; 8:18), but contemporary Mormons teach that three separate gods rule our planet and that all married Mormon males will themselves become gods!

Secondly, their book insists upon the necessity of the new birth (Mosiah 27:24-28; Alma 5:14), but today the necessity of water baptism is stressed as a precondition of salvation and the new birth.

Thirdly, the *Book of Mormon* teaches eternal glory or punishment, with no second chance of salvation beyond the grave (III Nephi 27:11-17; Mosiah 3:24-27; II Nephi 28:22,23; Alma 34:32-35), but we are now told by Mormons that almost everyone will enjoy some degree of glory and that proxy baptisms can release those people who go to the 'prison house' after death. Despite this inconsistency, Mormons try hard to commend their book as an authentic and final revelation from God.

However, two recent studies have again brought the *Book of Mormon* into disrepute. The family of the Mormon General Authority and apologist Brigham Roberts allowed scholars to examine two manuscripts which he wrote in 1922 and in which he argues cogently that Joseph Smith was probably the author of the *Book of Mormon*. In addition to this, there is a detailed study of the *Book of Mormon* by an ex-Mormon scholar, H. Michael Marquardt, in which he instances 200 quotations in the book from the Authorized Version of the Bible! Claims that their book is 'the most correct book on earth' and that 'An angel made fifteen trips from the throne of God to see that this *Book of Mormon* was properly translated and printed' are not confirmed by the real facts. Apart from the more compelling evidence it is true, for example, that nearly 4,000 changes have been made in their book since it was first published, that is, in the space of little more than 150 years! The Bible alone is the Word of God and as such it is trustworthy and powerful. Read the Bible and believe its teaching!

Is Mormon Christian?

The brief but accurate answer to this question is 'no'; the Mormon claim to be a fulfilled and restored expression of Christianity is a foolish one and certainly is unsupported by the facts. Both Mormonism and Christianity embrace very different doctrines of God, creation, humanity, salvation and the after-life.

Can a genuinely converted person remain within Mormonism? Again the answer must be a negative one for true Christians will want to be in a Bible-teaching church where they can be fed in the Word and fellowship with other Christians.

But what of a converted person becoming a Mormon? This is 'a scenario', we are told, 'that is becoming increasingly common'.[2] Such a person may be 'backslidden' but in the light of 1 John 2:19 may never have been genuinely converted to Christ. However in our 'highly syncretised world', Blomberg, a contibutor to the book mentioned earlier in the chapter (p.127), rightly fears that some truly 'born again' believers may be attempting to add Mormon beliefs to their Christian experience. Beware!

RELEVANT COMPARISONS

Mormons	The Bible
GOD	
Mormons believe God is Adam. God was once a mortal like ourselves but progressed to become an exalted being. There are many gods and the Trinity for them comprises three separate individuals who are physically distinct from each other.	'The LORD is God; besides him there is no other' (Deuteronomy 4:35). 'God is spirit, and his worshippers must worship in spirit and in truth' (John 4:24). 'For there is one God and one mediator between God and men, the man Christ Jesus' (1 Timothy 2:5). 'I the LORD do not change' (Malachi 3:6).

CREATION

Matter is eternal so God is not so much a Creator but rather a 'Shaper' and 'Organizer' of already existing matter.

The structure, context and message of Genesis 1:1 is that God created the universe out of nothing.

' '...Jesus Christ, through whom all things came...' (1 Corinthians 8:6).

'...God, who created all things' (Ephesians 3:9).

BIBLE

They believe that the *Book of Mormon* and the Bible have equal authority as the Word of God. They misuse Ezekiel 37:15-17, suggesting that 'the two sticks' referred to here are the Bible and the *Book of Mormon*. According to the Mormons, these become one stick, that is, God's Word. But verses 18-22 explain clearly that the sticks represent the tribes of Israel and Judah who together form one people.

Revelation for them is continuous and 'modern', for private revelations were given to Joseph Smith. In practice they neglect the Bible in preference for Smith's writings.

'All Scripture is God-breathed and is useful for teaching, rebuking, correcting and training in righteousness, so that the man of God may be thoroughly equipped for every good work' (2 Timothy 3:16-17).

'Above all, you must understand that no prophecy of Scripture came about by the prophet's own interpretation. For prophecy never had its origin in the will of man, but men spoke from God as they were carried along by the Holy Spirit' (2 Peter 1:20-21; cf. Revelation 22:18-19).

PERSON OF CHRIST

Mormons claim that Christ was a god like the humans and a

'In the beginning was the Word, and the Word was with God, and pre-existent spirit; in addition he was the brother of the devil and the son of Adam. He was not unique therefore in his nature or life, nor was his birth supernatural. They regard Christ as a polygamist who married both Mary and Martha at Cana of Galilee. Unmarried people and couples whose marriages are not 'sealed' in a Mormon temple can only become angels after death. Those 'sealed' for eternity become 'gods' — hence the importance for Mormons of Christ's being married.

the Word was God' (John 1:1).

'No one has ever seen God, but God the One and Only, who is at the Father's side, has made him known' (John 1:18).

'The Word became flesh and made his dwelling among us. We have seen his glory, the glory of the One and Only, who came from the Father, full of grace and truth' (John 1:14).

'His mother Mary was pledged to be married to Joseph, but before they came together, she was found to be with child through the Holy Spirit' (Matthew 1:18).

'The virgin will be with child and will give birth to a son, and will call him Immanuel' (Isaiah 7:14).

DEATH OF CHRIST

Since they regard man as being basically good and God as no more than an exalted man, there is no great problem in attaining salvation. There was no need for Christ to satisfy the justice of God on our behalf and his death dealt only

'Without the shedding of blood there is no forgiveness' (Hebrews 9:22).

'Therefore by the deeds of the law no flesh will be justified in his sight... But now the righteousness of God ... is revealed ... even the righteousness of God, with the sins of Adam and has no power to save us. Obedience to laws and Mormon ceremonies such as baptism is essential to salvation.

through faith in Jesus Christ, to all and on all who believe ... being justified freely by his grace through the redemption that is in Christ Jesus; whom God set forth as a propitiation by his blood, through faith' (Romans 3:20-25, NKJV).

'Look, the Lamb of God, who takes away the sin of the world!' (John 1:29).

'He himself bore our sins in his body on the tree' (1 Peter 2:24).

'But when this priest had offered for all time one sacrifice for sins, he sat down at the right hand of God' (Hebrews 10:12).

Mormons claim to have both the Aaronic and Melchizedekan priesthood.

Hebrews 7:12 shows the Aaronic priesthood is fulfilled by Christ; see also verse 24 which states that the Melchizedekan priesthood belongs to Christ ('unchangeable' in the AV in Greek means 'untransferable').

RESURRECTION OF CHRIST

Although it preceded others, his resurrection was in no way unique and was completely unrelated to our justification. Every man who is eventually made perfect and raised from the dead will become like the Father and Son in every respect.

'And if Christ has not been raised, your faith is futile; you are still in your sins' (1 Corinthians 15:17).

'He was delivered over to death for our sins, and was raised to life for our justification' (Romans 4:25).

Their claim that the risen Lord visited America in A.D. 34 has no historical support and is at variance with Acts 1:8-11 and other New Testament narratives.

'I am the resurrection and the life. He who believes in me will live, even though he dies; and whoever lives and believes in me will never die' (John 11:25-26).

HOLY SPIRIT

Mormons regard the Holy Spirit in impersonal terms, frequently referring to him as 'it', and describe him as a substance composed of individual, material particles. They deny his indispensable work in applying redemption to sinners and reject the indwelling of the Holy Spirit in believers. Only the Mormon priesthood can confer the Holy Spirit on people through the laying on of hands.

'When the Counsellor comes, whom I will send to you from the Father, the Spirit of truth, who goes out from the Father, he will testify about me' (John 15:26; cf. 14:26; 16:8, 13).

'...chosen according to the foreknowledge of God the Father, through the sanctifying work of the Spirit, for obedience to Jesus Christ and sprinkling by his blood' (1 Peter 1:1-2).

'Don't you know that you yourselves are God's temple and that God's Spirit lives in you' (1 Corinthians 3:16).

'The Spirit of him ... is living in you' (Romans 8:11).

'I will pour out my Spirit on all people' (Acts 2:17).

'Exalted to the right hand of God, he has received from the Father the promised Holy Spirit and has poured out what you now see and hear' (Acts 2:33).

MAN AND SIN

Misusing the words of Satan to Eve, 'You will be like God', Mormons promise the faithful that they will be gods. Man is therefore a potential god and God was once a man like us (Adam). All humans and spirits (including Christ and Satan) existed as spirit beings from eternity but at their physical birth these spirit beings are given bodies and their life on earth is a time of probation which determines the status and destiny of the individual after the resurrection.

According to the Mormons, the sin of Adam proved to be a great blessing to mankind for, apart from it, he would not have known good and evil nor had a posterity. Man is not a sinner by nature.

'The LORD God formed the man from the dust of the ground and breathed into his nostrils the breath of life, and the man became a living being' (Genesis 2:7; Romans 5:12-21).

'...for all have sinned and fall short of the glory of God' (Romans 3:23).

'The heart is deceitful above all things and is beyond cure' (Jeremiah 17:9; cf. 1 John 1:8, 10).

SALVATION

They reject the biblical doctrine of justification by faith and advocate faith plus works and baptism for salvation. A good life, the keeping of rules and baptism by immersion admin-

'For it is by grace you have been saved, through faith — and this not from yourselves, it is the gift of God — not by works, so that no one can boast' (Ephesians 2:8-9).

istered only by Mormons guarantee salvation.

From the age of eight upwards, baptism can wash away sins but without total immersion there is no pardon. On the basis of 1 Corinthians 15:29, they encourage people to be baptized by proxy on behalf of dead relatives and friends.

'Justified freely by his grace through the redemption that came by Christ Jesus' (Romans 3:24).

'However, to the man who does not work but trusts God who justifies the wicked, his faith is credited as righteousness' (Romans 4:5).

'He saved us, not because of righteous things we had done, but because of his mercy. He saved us through the washing of rebirth and renewal by the Holy Spirit' (Titus 3:5).

'The work of God is this: to believe in the one he has sent' (John 6:29; Acts 16:31).

FUTURE STATE

People have a chance to be saved even after death; that is the teaching of Mormonism. Baptism by proxy for all the dead of past ages who have not had the opportunity of responding to the Mormon gospel is obligatory upon all members.

They have a materialistic view of the 'celestial' glory which awaits their

'Just as man is destined to die once, and after that to face judgement' (Hebrews 9:27).

'Between us and you a great chasm has been fixed, so that those who want to go from here to you cannot, nor can anyone cross over from there to us' (Luke 16:26).

'If anyone's name was not found written in the

people; non-Mormons will be damned.

book of life, he was thrown into the lake of fire' (Revelation 20:15).

'...when the Lord Jesus is revealed from heaven in blazing fire with his powerful angels. He will punish those who do not know God and do not obey the gospel of our Lord Jesus. They will be punished with everlasting destruction and shut out from the presence of the Lord and from the majesty of his power...' (2 Thessalonians 1:7-9).

Mormons misuse 1 Corinthians 15:29 in support of their baptism by proxy for the dead. While there are as many as a hundred different interpretations of this verse, we should note the following points about it:

1. Paul is discussing in this chapter the resurrection of the dead and not baptism.
2. The verse does not say that baptism for the dead was practised by the Corinthian church nor acknowledged by them as a Christian rite.
3. Nevertheless it was practised in their area (although not in their church) so that Paul can appeal to this practice as something they had heard about.
4. I favour the following interpretation: Paul, intent on arguing and developing the doctrine of the general resurrection of the dead, is prepared here even to appeal to this pagan practice in the Corinth area

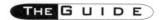

insomuch as it assumes the resurrection of the dead. In no way does Paul advocate baptism by proxy for the dead.

5. One important rule in interpreting the Bible is that we should interpret the obscure by the clear teaching of other passages. We must not build fanciful doctrines on obscure verses in the Bible.

THE GUIDE

CHAPTER FOURTEEN

CHRISTIAN SCIENCE

A BRIEF HISTORY

We now turn to a group known as Christian Science; or, to use the official title, the Church of Christ, Scientist. Their world headquarters is in Boston, Massachusetts, USA, where their 'Original Mother Church' was built in 1894. The group operates in seventy countries and has over 2,200 branch churches. Most of the 'churches' are found in English-speaking countries: the USA, Canada, UK and Ireland, Australia, New Zealand and South Africa. The next largest numbers are in German-speaking countries.

Different

But why call them a cult? They are different from the more intimidating and mind-controlling cults like Scientology and even some Exclusive Brethren groups. The point needs to be emphasized. For example, Christian Science rightly regards religious freedom as 'a fundamental right of all'. Nor do they seek to brainwash members and isolate them from society. They also insist that they do not use hypnotism, chants, rituals or esoteric practices. However, some ex-members have now concluded that the group is cultic but that it functions without many of the obvious controls, such as physical isolation and diet, used by other groups.

At this point, I am using the term 'cult' in relation to Christian Science in a primary sense, to refer to a serious deviation from orthodox, biblical Christianity. Sociologists are not so interested in this usage of the term because some of the typical and worrying cultic features such as brainwashing, exploitation, abuse, protest, withdrawal and violence are absent. My criterion for this primary use of the term 'cult' is, therefore, theological and biblical rather than sociological.

Another factor to be borne in mind is that Christian Science belongs to a group of older and more traditional cults like Christadelphians and Jehovah's Witnesses, which tend now to be accepted as harmless features of the religious scene.

Active propagation

Why, then, should we include Christian Science in this book? One reason is that there are many branches in the USA and the United Kingdom, and the movement is actively propagating its teaching, although, admittedly, it has been in decline for several years.

Some ex-members have grouped themselves together as United Christian Scientists. Despite these developments, the teaching of Christian Science has influenced individuals in Britain as well as in other countries.

Another reason for considering Christian Science is its indirect influence on certain areas of Pentecostalism and other groupings such as the 'Faith Movement'. Let me explain.

Names like Kenneth Copeland, Morris Cerullo, Benny Hinn, Frederick Price and Kenneth Hagin are well known in some circles. Sadly, their teachings are dubious and often heretical. Their major themes are faith, prosperity, wealth, healing, identification and 'revelation knowledge'. All the above persons recycle, in one form of another, the teaching of Hagin, commonly regarded as the founder of the Faith Movement. However, researchers like D. R. McConnell have shown conclusively that Hagin 'copied extensively' from the writings of E. W. Kenyon.

Ideas from Baker-Eddy

This point is important because the influences on Kenyon himself included that of Christian Science. There is ample evidence for this claim. John Kennington, for example, recalls a conversation in which Kenyon admitted he had freely used ideas from Mary Baker-Eddy, the founder of Christian Science. Ern Baxter, who knew Kenyon well in later years, also confirms that he was 'influenced' by Baker-Eddy's teaching.[1] In fact, Kenyon was 'widely read' concerning other related cults and ideas which are often classified under the title of New Thought.[2] And Kenyon also used the term 'spiritual scientist'.[3] There are links between New Thought, including Christian Science, and the contemporary Faith Movement. The following statement from Christian Science is alarming: 'In recent decades, a number of main-line Christian leaders have extracted the Christian Science concept of Divine Mind ... and grafted it on to traditional Christian belief.' That should concern us deeply.

History

How did Christian Science begin? The history of the cult centres around Mary Baker-Eddy (1821-1910). She was brought up by God-fearing Calvinistic parents who were members of a Congregationalist church in the USA. At an early age she rejected her parents' theology.

Constant ill-health, unpleasant periods of residence with friends and relatives, and the death of her first husband; together with deliberate estrangement from her only child and an extremely unhappy second marriage followed by divorce — all contributed to her anguish and disillusionment.

There were two incidents, in particular, which had a profound influence on her thinking. The first concerned a 'healing' which she supposedly experienced through Phineas Quimby. The latter's approach to 'healing' was essentially non-religious and auto-suggestive. A second incident was more important and occurred in 1866. This was when she fell on a frozen pavement and hurt herself. There are conflicting accounts concerning the extent of her injury, but Mary Baker-Eddy claims that at this time the principles of healing were revealed to her and she applied them for her own healing.

Church formed

Convinced that God had healed her, she spent several years reflecting on the subject and in 1875 expressed her understanding of the subject in *Science and Health with Key to the Scriptures*. Consistent with other cult founders, Mrs Baker-Eddy insisted that she was a unique channel of revelation and the custodian of the key for understanding the Bible. Misusing Revelation chapter 12, she claimed that she was the woman mentioned there and 'the God-appointed messenger to this age'. She is referred to as the 'Discoverer, Founder, and Leader of Christian Science'.

In 1879 Mrs Baker-Eddy and a group of followers agreed to 'organize a church ... which should reinstate primitive Christianity and its lost element of healing'. This 'church' was reorganized in 1892.

Each local group is democratically governed and 'is a lay church in which every member had equal standing...' There are no ministers and they prefer to 'turn to prayer and these two books [the Bible and *Science and Health*] for counsel and healing'. They claim that more than 50,000 authenticated testimonies of healing have been published in their periodicals during the past 112 years, with medical verification of some of them.

Assessment

I must warn you that their teachings are far removed from those of the Bible. For example, in their view God is not a person but merely Mind and the universe an extension of this Mind. In denying Christ's deity, they insist that Jesus Christ died only to show the unreality of death. 'Salvation' is, they assert, gradual and continuous, evidenced through healing. These ideas represent major denials of biblical teaching and need to be challenged.

Reading the Bible

There are some ex-members who are now actively challenging the cult, both on biblical and theological grounds. Linda Stecher Kramer is one such person. She spent the first thirty years of her life in Christian Science and was committed to the group. In her early thirties she felt a deep sense of need to study the Bible without using *Science and Health*. Providentially, she met a Christian family at this time who witnessed to her concerning the central themes of Christianity. Sadly, the message seemed ridiculous to her and naive.

However, Linda continued reading the Bible and several months later had another discussion with her Christian friends about Christianity. They urged her to keep on reading the Bible. And then, soon, God met with her. Reading Romans 3:23-25 she reports, 'Everything my friends had said seemed to be wrapped up in that one passage. I suddenly realised that Jesus had not gone to the cross to prove the unreality of sin, disease and death, but to *pay* for my sins. "For *all* have sinned..." ... I caught a glimmer of truth.'

In a footnote to Christian Scientists, Linda emphasizes that the original Greek words for 'redemption' and 'atonement' (or propitiation) in Romans 3 involve payment for sins and reconciliation with God. She adds, 'Atonement deals with restoring a broken relationship with God rather than referring to a pre-existing "at-one-ment" with Him.'

Within a short time she had trusted in the Lord Jesus Christ. 'Finally,' she testifies, 'I had to concede that Christian Science contradicts the Bible rather than elucidates it. I had no choice but to leave.'

Significant date

Another significant date in the history of Christian Science is 6 January 1895. On that day the

'Discoverer and Founder of Christian Science', Mary Baker-Eddy, gave a 'Dedicatory Sermon' in her rather lavish 'First Church' in Boston, Massachusetts. The occasion? 2600 children had given generously towards a room in the building for their leader. Baker-Eddy wanted to acknowledge their contribution and seized the opportunity to commend her teachings.

This 'Dedicatory Sermon' was published with some favourable press reports under the title *Pulpit and Press*. The biblical text misused by her in the sermon was Psalm 36:8. Her foolish claim was that her teachings concerning God or Mind uniquely 'satisfy' people.

There are some interesting references in the sermon to her movement and influence. For example, she reports that in 1893 her 'form of prayer' (p.4) was used in the public sessions of the World's Parliament of Religions.

Again, referring to her *Science and Health with Key to the Scriptures* first published in 1875, Baker-Eddy claimed twenty years later that it 'is in its ninety-first edition of one thousand copies'. That is not all.

'It is in the public libraries of the principal cities, colleges and universities of America; also the same in Great Britain, France, Germany, Russia, Italy, Greece, Japan, India and China; in Oxford University and the Victoria Institute, England, in the Academy of Greece and the Vatican at Rome' (p.5). The claim illustrates the extensive distribution, as well as reception, of *Science and Health* in this period.

Great expectations

Mrs Baker-Eddy had great expectations for the continued success of her book: 'I predict', she said, 'that in the twentieth century every Christian church in our land [USA], and a few in far-off lands, will approximate the understanding of Christian Science ... and Christendom will be classified as Christian Scientists' (p.14). Thankfully, that has not happened, although the influence of the cult's teaching on sections of Christendom has been more extensive than we have appreciated.

In this sermon, Baker-Eddy provides two interesting examples of the way in which her teaching had affected church leaders. One relates to a nonconformist minister in Boston, Rev. William R. Alger, whom she describes as a 'brilliant enunciator, seeker and servant of Truth'. He gave considerable encouragement to Mary Baker-Eddy. On one occasion he told a group of Boston intellectuals, 'You may find in Mrs Baker-Eddy's metaphysical teachings more than is dreamt of in your philosophy' (pp.5-6).

Another person influenced by Baker-Eddy was the wife of a Protestant missionary. The woman's name is withheld but she is quoted as saying, 'I went with my husband, a missionary, to China in 1884. He went out under the auspices of the Methodist Episcopal Church. I feel "the truth" is leading us to return to Japan.'

Baker-Eddy explains that the woman had written to her in 1894 with news that she had received a copy of *Science and Health* only six months previously. 'I had not read three pages before I realised,' she explained to Baker-Eddy, 'I had found that for which I had hungered since girlhood, and was healed instantaneously... I cast from me the false remedy I had vainly used and turned to the "great Physician".' It is sad that a woman involved in Protestant missionary work in Asia should have been taken in by Baker-Eddy's teaching. But she was deceived and commended these heretical ideas to others in subsequent years.

Final revelation?

Concerning her book *Science and Health*, Baker-Eddy emphasizes in the Dedicatory Sermon that it is 'the leaven fermenting religion ... it is the upheaval produced when Truth is neutralising error and impurities are passing off...' (p.5). In the same sermon she adds, 'I have ordained the Bible and the Christian Science textbook, *Science and Health with Key to the Scriptures*, as pastor of The First Church of Christ, Scientist, in Boston' (p.6). In other words, rejecting the system of local pastors she governs each group through her own misguided interpretation of the Bible.

Baker-Eddy regarded her book *Science and Health* as special; in fact, she describes it as 'this final revelation of the absolute divine Principle of scientific mental healing' (107:1-6).

How did she receive this 'final revelation'? Her answer is, 'through divine revelation, reason and demonstration ... through Divine Power' (109:20-23). According to Baker-Eddy, while the Bible has many 'mistakes' (139:15-22) and contradictions (522:3-5), her own book is 'uncontaminated' (457:1-2) and constitutes 'the voice of Truth to this age' (456:27-28). While her textbook is alleged to be 'a companion to the Bible', in practice it functions as the dominant, authoritative text and the unique 'key' to the Bible.

Similar claims are made by other cults, of course, as books written by various cult leaders are elevated to levels of infallibility and supremacy. Despite their respect for the Bible, *Science and Health* is regarded by Christian Scientists as 'the final word'.

Crucial point

Katie Bretz challenges Christian Scientists at this crucial point of the authority and sufficiency of the Bible. After being a cult member for over twenty years, 'supported and spurred on by numerous physical healings', she finally became a Christian through reading the Bible alone. 'God worked in my life to draw me to Him — to have a vital, intimate relationship with the Lord Jesus Christ — and I was saved,' she testifies. 'It was like walking through a door.'

Excitedly, Bretz warns Christian Scientists: 'You need [to] stop the Christian Science filtering when you read the Bible. Put on and look through the glasses of [the] gospel — see the simplicity inherent in Christ.' And she adds, 'I've learned that salvation is everything. What is a healing of cancer if it keeps you away from knowing the Lord Jesus Christ, and being saved? It's a smoke screen.'

The challenge to read the Bible alone and without Baker-Eddy's heretical commentary is renewed by Katie Bretz. The Bible, she insists, 'is God's Word. His Word is self-consistent' and sufficient '*without* the filters of Christian Science'. On her web page she writes: 'I urge you to read Paul's writings with an open heart. You need to read more of the Bible, have less filtering, and let it speak to you *alone*.'

In the closing part of her testimony, Bretz emphasizes that the Bible 'has changed my life forever... I read the Bible with new understanding and feel the love of the Father, Son and Holy Ghost.' Then, in conclusion, she declares, 'So much awaits you! Christian Science doesn't even touch 1% of what God is, or what He's given you. "Waxed fruit and mud pies" are what you find in Christian Science!'

Uneasy reflection

Another testimony to the power and sufficiency of the Bible is provided by Stanley D. Meyers who was considered to be a 'successful Christian Scientist', exemplifying the doctrines of Mary Baker-Eddy. He was ambitious, too, achieving some of the top positions in the cult, especially in Akron, Ohio.

Providentially, Meyers and his wife started attending some home Bible studies conducted by Christians. He was impressed by their Bible knowledge but realized rather painfully that the teachings of Christian Science were in direct conflict with the Bible. An uneasy period of reflection followed as he tried to remain faithful to Mary Baker-Eddy. But it was in vain. He concluded that 'the teachings of Christian Science and the teachings of the Bible cannot both be true'.

Unexpectedly, one day as he was driving to work, he reports that, 'an absolute heart conviction overwhelmed me that the Bible is the Word of God. It is not a book written by men about God but a book written by God. The Bible is not a book by man seeking a lost God but a book about God seeking lost men. I could therefore believe every word in the Bible,' he insists, 'because it was God's declaration to men.'

And the result? Well, through the Bible and the Bible alone, he came to trust in Christ as Saviour and Lord. Why not read the Bible alone and, like Meyers, find the true and living God?

Before we look in more detail at what Christian Science teaches and believes I want to make five introductory points in order to approach the subject responsibly.

First, Christian Science beliefs are expressed clearly in many books and pamphlets as well as on their own web site. There is an abundance of data available.

Second, their special appeal is to Mrs Baker-Eddy's *Science and Health with Key to the Scriptures*. All their beliefs were expressed by their leader in this book. They foolishly claim that Baker-Eddy is the unique revealer of Christ, the Truth, in this age so that *Science and Health* is the final revelation which correctly explains 'true Christianity'.

Third, in describing their beliefs our aim is to evaluate them in the light of the Bible. That alone must be our criterion for establishing whether a teaching is true or false. The Bible is the one and only objective standard by which we must ascertain truth. As we will see, Christian Science teaching must be rejected as false because it contradicts the clear teaching of the Bible.

Sincerely wrong

Fourth, Christian Scientists are sincere in holding to their beliefs and practising them. Those members whom I have met have been charming, as well as sincere in thinking that they have the 'truth'.

The fifth point is related, namely, that although Christian Scientists are sincere, they are sincerely wrong! To be sincere is not enough in itself. And even Christians need to grasp the point. For example, we may sincerely believe that the visitor at the door is a political canvasser or a genuine telephone company representative. But the man is not what he claims to be. In fact, he only wants to enter our home to steal our money and possessions. Sincere people can be sincerely wrong. And sincerity is not the criterion of truth although, of course, those who believe the truth of the Bible should be sincere and genuine.

Bible doctrine

What we are discussing, then, is doctrine, especially Bible doctrine. But the term 'doctrine' still has a bad press, even among Christians. If you associate doctrine with awkward and extreme doctrinaire individuals or groups, then you may want to shy away from it.

Perhaps you associate 'doctrine' with a past age. You may feel it is an anachronism early in a new millennium to be concerned over ancient creedal formulations concerning the Holy Trinity, for example, or Reformation principles like the sufficiency and supremacy of Scripture, or justification by faith alone. After all, in a 'post-modernist' society there are supposed to be no absolutes in either morals or doctrine.

But such an attitude towards doctrine is wrong, for it strikes at the foundations of the Christian faith. There is such a thing as truth. And that is what the Bible is — ultimate, absolute and infallible truth from God, who is himself the source of all truth.

This is why we are going to compare the teaching of Christian Science with what the Bible says on basic doctrines. But before we do so, I want to say a little more concerning their views of God and Christ. These are key subjects which we need to understand from God's Word, both for our own benefit as Christians and in order to help unbelievers.

The doctrine of God

The doctrine of God is a fundamental teaching and one which determines other doctrines. Here we note that Christian Science has a radically different view of God from that revealed in the Bible.

At first glance, however, their official statement seems orthodox: 'God, Spirit, is the supreme Being … ever-present, all-knowing, all-powerful and wholly good.' But what are they really saying? Their explanation is revealing: 'God's nature is seen through synonymous names for God used or implied in the Bible, including divine Mind, Spirit, Soul, Principle, Life, Truth, Love.' In other words, Christian Scientists do not believe that God is a person or that he is distinct from the universe. For them, God is only Intelligence or Mind, the All-in-all. Mind is all that exists.

Furthermore, they teach that there is no reality or existence outside of this Mind or God. The technical terms for this position are pantheism (the belief that the universe and God are identical) and monism (all is one).

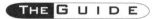

Far-reaching implications

Notice the devastating implications of their view of God. Firstly, God is the universe and we are all part of the one divine reality or Mind. But the Bible distinguishes clearly between the nature of God and creation: 'you laid the foundations of the earth, and the heavens are the work of your hands. They will perish, but you remain…' (Psalm 102:25-26). What is more, the world is preserved by God continually: 'For by him all things were created: things in heaven and on earth, visible and invisible … all things were created by him and for him … in him all things hold together' (Colossians 1:16-17). And while God is present everywhere and active in the universe he created, nevertheless he is also wholly 'other', distinct and apart from the universe. God is 'the high and lofty One … he who lives for ever, whose name is holy' (Isaiah 57:15).

Secondly, according to Christian Science, God is impersonal, and this involves the denial of the Holy Trinity of divine persons — Father, Son and Holy Spirit. In fact they claim that the Holy Spirit is 'Divine Science' which the group regards as 'the universal expression of Christian Science'!

The claim is obviously wrong. God is revealed in the Bible as a triune personal God; and within the one Godhead, there are three distinct, eternal and co-equal persons (see Matthew 28:19; 2 Corinthians 13:14). The Holy Spirit is the third eternal person in the Godhead whom the Lord Jesus refers to with personal pronouns (John 14:16-17; 16:7-14). The Spirit has a mind (John 15:26), a will (1 Corinthians 12:11) and both speaks and teaches (1 Timothy 4:1; Acts 13:2; Luke 12:12). These are just a few of the Bible statements which indicate the personality of the Holy Spirit.

All in the mind?

Thirdly, if Christian Science is right, all matter is an illusion and has no real existence. Only the Divine Mind exists, along with its ideas! This involves the denial of man's physical nature, so that he has no bones, flesh or blood. They also teach that man is perfect because sin and evil are unreal, being merely errors of mortal mind. The theology of Christian Science is similar to the Docetic-Gnostic teaching in early church history, which separated the spiritual from the 'evil' material realm. Both maintain that Spirit and matter do not and cannot mix; for Christian Science, however, the reason is not that matter is evil but rather that it does not exist.

To deny the reality of matter, sickness or death, however, is to fly in the face of the evidence. And the Bible teaches that God who is spirit (John 4:24) also created all matter (Genesis 1:1-31) and saw that it was 'very good'. Man also fell into real sin (Genesis 3; Romans 5:12-19) and 'all have sinned and fall short of the glory of God' (Romans 3:23). Suffering and death are the consequences of God's just punishment of sin.

The doctrine of Jesus Christ

According to Christian Science, Jesus was a fallible human, a divine idea. He shows the way to salvation but is himself unable to save. Jesus was not God incarnate, nor was he the Christ. The only reason for the cross was to show the unreality of death. Such are the errors taught by Christian Science concerning the Lord Jesus Christ.

In contrast, the Bible clearly teaches that Jesus is true man (Philippians 2:7) but also fully God: 'For in Christ all the fulness of the Deity lives in bodily form' (Colossians 2:9). Peter too was commended for proclaiming, 'You are the Christ, the Son of the living God' (Matthew 16:16). And rather than being merely a 'Way-shower', Jesus is himself 'the way' (John 14:6).

Christian Science continues to strike at the heart of the Christian gospel. They say that Jesus did not die. The Bible, however, insists that 'Christ died'. It was a real death. And Jesus prophesied that he would die and then be raised from death (Matthew 12:38-40; 16:21). He died, also, 'for our sins according to the Scriptures' (1 Corinthians 15:3). But that is not the end. Christ also 'was raised on the third day according to the Scriptures' (v. 4). A real physical resurrection from the dead! And 'if Christ has not been raised, your faith is futile; you are still in your sins ... we are to be pitied more than all men' (vv. 17, 19).

The glorious news of the gospel proclaims, 'But Christ has indeed been raised from the dead' (v. 20), and he alone is the one who is able to save us. I appeal to Christian Scientists who read this chapter to embrace in faith the Christ revealed in the Bible.

Miracles

Healing is important for this cult because they believe it proves its 'absolute and divine' origin and nature.[4] While not denying that God can work miracles today, the biblical principle is clear. Miracles, including healings, were not performed indiscriminately in biblical times, but only for specific reasons and to attest key stages in salvation history. They are uncommon today; indeed, it is extremely difficult to find convincing evidence that many of the so-called miracles today are genuine.

A healing, therefore, is not necessarily the work of God. The Bible declares that the devil and his hosts are able to work signs and healing miracles (Exodus 7:10-11, 20-22; 8:6-7; 2 Corinthians 11:13-15; 2 Thessalonians 2:9-10; Revelation 13:12-14; 16:14).

Whether or not healings reported by Christian Science are merely psychologically-induced or are the work of evil powers is open to discussion but the cult places too much importance on healing. 'What is a healing of cancer', asks Katie Bretz, 'if it keeps you away from knowing the Lord Jesus Christ, and being saved? It's a smoke screen (see Matthew 7:21-23)'. Such alleged healings as reported by them can mask spiritual hunger and disillusionment.

Failed attempts

However, there is another side to the practice of healing in this cult, namely, failed attempts to heal. For example, Dr Rita Swan was a former Christian Scientist whose son died as a result of the family's reliance on the cult's teaching. In a useful pamphlet entitled *Cry, the Beloved Children*,[5] Dr Swan documents some failed healings in Christian Science that have cost children (and adults) their lives. The author helps to expose the fact that Christian Science healing is not as effective as people have been led to believe.

Caroline Fraser has also provided an in-depth study of 'child cases', and of some other problems facing the Christian Science movement, in an article entitled 'Suffering Children and the Christian Science Church'.[6]

Amongst some faithful adherents there is a preference for competent medical treatment, even though official policy condemns the use of drugs such as aspirins and antibiotics yet allows immunizations, obstetric care at childbirth and treatment of broken bones. To replace medical treatment they advocate 'prayer and mental renewal' and, for a charge, they provide their own 'practitioner' to encourage people to avoid reliance on medics.

RELEVANT COMPARISONS

Christian Science	The Bible
GOD	
God is substance and the only intelligence in the universe. He is the All-in-all and there is no reality or existence outside of him. God is also divine Mind and mind is all that exists. This teaching is pantheism, namely, the theory that the universe is God and God is the universe. The Trinity is also rejected.	'The heavens, even the highest heaven, cannot contain you' (1 Kings 8:27). 'Before the mountains were born or you brought forth the earth and the world, from everlasting to everlasting you are God' (Psalm 90:2). 'They will perish, but you remain; they will all wear out like a garment. Like clothing you will change them and they will be discarded. But you remain the same, and your years will never end' (Psalm 102:26-27).

BIBLE

While they claim to take the inspired word of the Bible as their 'sufficient guide to eternal life', in practice they only accept the Bible as interpreted by Mrs Eddy, and her *Science and health, with Key to the Scriptures* is their ultimate authority. Furthermore, the Bible is thought to have errors, whereas the writings of Mrs Eddy are 'unerring and divine'.

'For I trust in thy word' (Psalm 119:42).

'Thy word is very pure... Of old I have known from thy testimonies, that thou hast founded them for ever' (Psalm 119:140, 152, AV).

'To the law and to the testimony: if they speak not according to this word, it is because there is no light in them' (Isaiah 8:20, AV).

'Scripture cannot be broken' (John 10:35).

PROVIDENCE

God, having no existence apart from the universe, cannot plan or decree events or govern the world.

As neither God nor bread exist independently of each other, they deny the validity, for example, of the petition, 'Give us this day our daily bread.' Using her 'key' to reinterpret the petition, Mrs Eddy explains it as 'Give us grace for today; feed our familiar affections.'

'I have rejected him as king over Israel... I am sending you to Jesse... I have chosen one of his sons to be king' (1 Samuel 16:1).

'The king's heart is in the hand of the LORD; he directs it like a watercourse wherever he pleases' (Proverbs 21:1).

'He does as he pleases with the powers of heaven and the peoples of the earth' (Daniel 4:35).

'...according to the plan of him who works out everything in conformity with the purpose of his will' (Ephesians 1:11).

MAN

To say 'Matter does not exist' means in relation to man that he has no body. Belief in bodies is an error of the mortal mind. Man is spiritual and the reflection of God.

In denying man's fall into sin they also teach that evil, sin and matter are unreal, so when we think we sin or see others sin we are being deluded by our mortal minds. If, then, man has no separate mind from God, it means that man is a part of God and the distinction between creature and Creator is rejected.

'The LORD God formed the man from the dust of the ground and breathed into his nostrils the breath of life, and the man became a living being' (Genesis 2:7).

'...and the dust returns to the ground it came from, and the spirit returns to God who gave it' (Ecclesiastes 12:7).

'Therefore, just as sin entered the world through one man, and death through sin, and in this way death came to all men, because all sinned...' (Romans 5:12).

'If we claim to be without sin, we deceive ourselves and the truth is not in us' (1 John 1:8).

PERSON OF CHRIST

A distinction is made between Jesus, a merely human man who lived in Palestine nearly 2,000 years ago, and Christ, which is the name for the divine idea. Christ, then, is not a person, but only an idea, and this idea continues in the teaching of Christian Science!

Jesus (Saviour) is the personal name of the Lord, whereas Christ ('anointed one') is his official name as Messiah.

'The virgin will be with child and will give birth to a son, and they will call him Immanuel, which means "God with us"' (Isaiah 7:14; Matthew 1:23).

'The Word became flesh, and made his dwelling among us' (John 1:14).

'For I did not speak of my own accord, but the Father who sent me commanded me what to say and how to say it' (John 12:49).

'For in Christ all the fulness of the Deity lives in bodily form' (Colossians 2:9).

DEATH OF CHRIST

Jesus did not actually suffer or die. His death was only apparent and during his three days in the tomb he was alive. Thus his physical resurrection and ascension to heaven are denied.

Regarding sin as unreal, they view as abhorrent the teaching that the Lord atoned for our sin by the offering up of himself as our substitute on the cross. Rather he came to demonstrate a divine idea and his crucifixion demonstrated goodness and affection. His work was essentially that of providing us with an example to follow.

'How foolish you are, and how slow of heart to believe all that the prophets have spoken! Did not the Christ have to suffer these things and then enter his glory?' (Luke 24:25-26).

'...that Christ died for our sins according to the Scriptures, that he was buried, that he was raised on the third day' (1 Corinthians 15:3-4).

'Christ Jesus came into the world to save sinners' (1 Timothy 1:15).

'...Christ suffered for you... When they hurled their insults at him, he did not retaliate ... He himself bore our sins in his body on the tree...' (1 Peter 2:21, 23-24).

SALVATION

Man is not a sinner, so salvation from sin is unnecessary. But Mrs Eddy and her followers do speak of 'salvation', namely, salvation from false beliefs, so that a person is saved when he stops believing there is such a thing as sin. The death of Christ is entirely unrelated to salvation.

'God was reconciling the world to himself in Christ, not counting men's sins against them' (2 Corinthians 5:19).

'For there is one God and one mediator between God and men, the man Christ Jesus, who gave himself as a ransom for all men' (1 Timothy 2:5-6).

DEATH

Death is an illusion. There is an afterlife when the mind continues in a conscious state of existence which is a time of probation for everyone. Here spiritual 'growth' is necessary for all because even after death some errors and sins remain in our consciousness.

'You turn men back to dust, saying, "Return to dust, O sons of men."... The length of our days is seventy years ... for they quickly pass, and we fly away' (Psalm 90:3, 10).

'Just as man is destined to die once, and after that to face judgement' (Hebrews 9:27).

HOLY SPIRIT

Christian Science is regarded as the Holy Spirit. To receive the Holy Spirit means to have a greater understanding of Christian Science.

'The Spirit told Philip, "Go to that chariot and stay near it"' (Acts 8:29; cf. 16:7).

'And if the Spirit of him who raised Jesus from the dead is living in you, he who raised Christ from the dead will also give life to your mortal bodies through his Spirit, who lives in you' (Romans 8:11).

HELL AND HEAVEN

Perfection is the goal for those who progress after death, but if people remain in error they will be 'self-annihilated'. Apart from the fire of a guilty conscience, there is no hell; heaven is not a place but a divine state of mind.

'Rather, be afraid of the one who can destroy both soul and body in hell' (Matthew 10:28).

'Then they will go away to eternal punishment, but the righteous to eternal life' (Matthew 25:46).

'In my Father's house are many rooms; if it were not so, I would have told you. I am going there to prepare a place for you' (John 14:2).

DEVIL

It is a great mistake to believe in good and evil spirits. There is no personal devil.

'Satan entered into him' (John 13:27).

'Your enemy the devil prowls around like a roaring lion looking for someone to devour. Resist him, standing firm in the faith' (1 Peter 5:8-9).

SECOND COMING OF CHRIST

The personal return of the Lord Jesus is interpreted by them as the birth and development of Christian Science. Mrs Eddy refers to a Bible expositor who, on the basis of prophecies in Daniel, fixed 1866-67

'This same Jesus, who has been taken from you into heaven, will come back in the same way you have seen him go into heaven' (Acts 1:11).

'Why should any of you consider it incredible that

for the return of Christ, which 'happened' to be the years when she discovered Christian Science! Our Lord's personal and visible return in glory, the general physical resurrection of the body and final judgement are all denied by this cult.

God raises the dead?' (Acts 26:8).

'No one knows about that day or hour, not even the angels in heaven, nor the Son, but only the Father ... keep watch, because you do not know on what day your Lord will come' (Matthew 24:36, 42).

THE GUIDE

CHAPTER FIFTEEN

RASTAFARIANS

A BRIEF HISTORY

The total number of people following this movement is believed by some to be over one million worldwide. By contrast, a 1995 statistic estimates there were only 180,000 members worldwide.[1] In Jamaica itself, six out of ten Jamaicans are thought to be Rastafarians or sympathizers. In the United Kingdom there are about two million West Indians and an increasing number of them are responding to the gospel. One problem facing the growing number of West Indian churches is the activity of Rastafarians, who pose a serious threat to the work of the gospel among West Indian young people.

From 1975 to the present day, the Rastafarian movement has experienced astonishing growth. This is mainly attributed to the late Bob Marley, a Reggae musician, and the worldwide acceptance of Reggae as an avenue of Rastafarian self-expression. Marley became a prophet in the movement in 1975 and then its message spread quickly to the Caribbean and attracted the black youth in the islands.

Rastafarians are easily recognizable in our cities, with their uncut hair combed into long braids, and they usually wear a multi-coloured hat of red, green, black and gold. The colours are significant for they are the colours of Ethiopia.

The historical background

Why Ethiopia? Over seventy years ago, Marcus Garvey, an American black national and originally from Jamaica, tried to form a 'back to Africa' movement in the hope that this would result in the establishment of an independent African country largely consisting of Americans with African ancestry. Garvey had prophesied as well: 'Look to Africa where a black king shall be crowned, for the day of deliverance is near.'[2] In 1930 Ras Tafari succeeded to the throne of Ethiopia as Emperor Haile Selassie. His appointment gave new hope to many frustrated and economically poor Jamaicans who slowly recognized the emperor as their messiah and 'King of kings'.

The emperor's death in 1975 stunned many Jamaicans for they considered him to be the living god who had come in fulfilment of the prophesy. Rastafarians believe in the continued life of Selassie, but in a different realm, and they worship him as a god. Many Rastafarians reject Christianity and tend to view it as a 'white religion' while Western culture is deemed to be the modern 'Babylon'.

They also regard Africa, Ethiopia especially, as the 'Promised Land' of the Old Testament and that they themselves are the genuine descendants of David.

Rastafarian beliefs and practices

Despite their often untidy appearance, Rastafarians are told to live a respectable, moral life. Immorality, for example, as well as stealing, lying and the use of alcohol, are all forbidden but in order to meditate their followers are encouraged to smoke marijuana or 'ganja'. They do not have established churches or buildings.

This movement was built on, and fuelled by, hatred for white people, although there is evidence that many of their followers are not racists like the earlier members of the movement. By contrast, God's command is that we must love our neighbours, whoever they are (Matthew 5:43-44). It is only by the work of God in our hearts in the new birth that we are able to love people, for love is a fruit of the Spirit (Galatians 5:22; 2 Corinthians 5:17).

RELEVANT COMPARISONS

Rastafarians	The Bible
BIBLE	
Black people wrote the Bible exclusively for blacks.	'For prophecy never had its origin in the will of man, but men spoke from God as they were carried along by the Holy Spirit' (2 Peter 1:21). 'All Scripture is God-breathed and is useful for teaching, rebuking,

correcting and training in righteousness, so that the man of God may be thoroughly equipped for every good work' (2 Timothy 3:16-17).

GOD

Many Rastafarians believe that Haile Selassie is both God and Saviour.

'Before me no god was formed, nor will there be one after me. I, even I, am the LORD; and apart from me there is no saviour' (Isaiah 43:10-11).

INCARNATION

In the Emperor Haile Selassie, not Jesus, God became man. Jesus has been misrepresented by whites as a European. All the early Christians and Jesus were dark-skinned.

'But when the time had fully come, God sent his Son, born of a woman, born under law, to redeem those under law, that we might receive the full rights of sons' (Galatians 4:4-5; Philippians 2:6-8).

'Whoever believes that Jesus is the Christ is born of God...' (1 John 5:1).

SALVATION

Salvation and freedom will be realized only when black people return to Africa, from where they were originally taken as slaves by white slave traders.

'Salvation is found in no one else, for there is no other name under heaven given to men by which we must be saved' (Acts 4:12; cf. Galatians 1:4).

DEVIL

All white people are demons and belong to the devil.

By nature we are *all* slaves of sin (John 8:34) and belong to the devil (v. 44) but we are transferred to the kingdom of God when we trust in Christ (1 Peter 2:9-10; Colossians 1:13-14).

LIFE AFTER DEATH

Reincarnation is a popular and common belief among Rastafarians.

'Just as man is destined to die once, and after that to face judgement' (Hebrews 9:27).

CHAPTER SIXTEEN

THE UNIFICATION CHURCH: MOONIES

A BRIEF HISTORY

In 1954, at the age of thirty-four, Rev. Sun Myung Moon founded the Unification Church in Korea. Moon's parents were Presbyterians and gave him a religious upbringing, but at an early age he manifested a deep interest in spiritism, and when only sixteen he claimed his first occult experience. While praying on Easter Sunday 1936 he claims to have seen Jesus Christ, who revealed that Moon 'was destined to accomplish a great mission in which Jesus Christ would work with him'.

He read the Bible regularly and then went to Japan to study electrical engineering. At the end of the Second World War, he joined an extreme Pentecostal movement in Pyong Yang which emphasized private mystical revelations and also the imminent appearance of a new messiah who would be a Korean. One of his key spiritistic experiences occurred in 1945. Describing this encounter in his book *Divine Principle*, he claims to have 'fought alone against myriads of satanic forces, both in the spirit and physical world and finally triumphed over them all'. From this time, according to Moon, he became 'the absolute victor of heaven and earth … and the Lord of creation … the whole spirit world bowed down to him'.

For reasons which are somewhat obscure, he was imprisoned in North Korea but was released when General MacArthur, at the head of the United Nations forces, occupied his area. Moving to the south, Moon established his church in Seoul in 1954, calling it the Holy Spirit Association for the Unification of World Christianity. That same year when his first wife left him, Moon remarked, 'She did not understand my religion.' A year later he was again imprisoned, but this time in South Korea, charged with avoiding military duties and later with adultery and immoral practices. The charges, however, were not proven.

It is likely that Moon has been married four times. He married his present wife, Hak Ja Han, in 1960 and Moon describes this marriage as 'the marriage of the lamb', regarding their eight children as sinless because they are children of the messiah.

Success for Moon

1957 saw the publication of the *Divine Principle*, described as the 'key to the Scriptures', which records Moon's teachings in Korea to his followers. Rev. Moon became a successful businessman in Korea, amassing considerable wealth from pharmaceutical products, tea and rifles, among other things. *The Times* of 30 April 1978 headlined their overseas report on Moon as 'Founder of Unification Church but better known in Korea as owner of weapons factories'. Their reporter in Seoul, Peter Hazelhurst, says, 'Moon owns one factory in the new Chang-won Industrial complex near Pusan which makes defence equipment classified as secret and another in Sutack Ri, twenty-one miles north-east of Seoul, which is an air-gun factory. His other businesses include Korea's largest exporter of ginseng products (White Fire Company), whose annual exports to Japan alone are worth five million pounds.'[1] Moon's personal fortune was then estimated at eight million pounds.[2]

According to Moon, God 'appeared' to him in January 1972 telling him to prepare America for the Messiah's second coming. His subsequent activities in the States in the early mid-seventies were successful. In addition to winning many converts to his religion, he had meetings with Presidents Eisenhower and Nixon and supported Nixon during the Watergate scandal.

In 1975 the work of the movement was expanded as missionaries were sent out to ninety-five countries and it claims to have a total of three million members in at least 120 countries. However, Professor Tak Myung-Hwan of the Korea Theological Seminary believes this figure is grossly exaggerated. Possibly as part of their 'heavenly deception' (the belief that deception is justified in the propagating of Moon's teachings) they claim, for example, 360,000 supporters in Korea, but Professor Tak puts the figure at 10,000.[3] As a result of a poor public 'image' in the 1980s and 1990s both in America and Europe, due to charges of 'brainwashing' and 'isolating' young people from parents, the movement appeared to be on the wane, with a number of groups and individuals in the USA offering (for a fee) to 'kidnap' and 'deprogramme' Moonies in order to rehabilitate them to normal family and social life. However, the cult is now gaining ground.

To quote Professor Tak again, 'Moon claims he is the new Messiah, superior to Buddha, Jesus and Confucius. The Unification Church has never been a Christian church. It is a cult. And it puts Korea to shame before the world.' A similar pronouncement was made by the National Council of Churches of Christ in the USA in 1977: 'It cannot be considered as a Christian church.' What is even more important, the religion of Rev. Moon stands condemned as false by the Word of God.

The *Daily Mail* court case

Early in 1981 the Unification Church lost the longest and most expensive libel case in British legal history and was ordered to pay costs estimated at nearly one million pounds. Dennis Orme, leader of Sun Myung Moon's church in Britain, claimed damages against the *Daily Mail* for an article in 1978 that accused the church of brainwashing converts and breaking up families.

The allegations against the church were as follows:

1. They establish control over recruits with 'sophisticated mind-control techniques', developed from those used by the Chinese Communists in the Korean war, including extremely low-protein diets, sleep deprivation, 'love-bombing' and increasing blood sugar levels in order to muddle the brain — a technique called 'sugar-buzzing'.
2. The trademark of a recruit was a 'perpetual vapid smile' and a vacant glassy look.
3. Recruits were 'programmed as soldiers in a vast, fund-raising army, with no goals or ideals except as followers of the half-baked ravings of Moon, who lives in splendour while his followers lived in forced penury'.
4. Their motivation was just as strong as, if not stronger than, that of Communists.
5. The church raised vast funds by deceiving the public.

The jury, who took five hours to reach their verdict and heard evidence from more than 100 witnesses for over six months, decided that the *Daily Mail* was justified in its accusations. They made two recommendations:

1. They urged that the charitable status of the Unification Church should be examined by

the Inland Revenue on the grounds that it was really a political organization.
2. They expressed their deep compassion for all the young people still in the group.

Developments

The Moonies took several years in the United Kingdom to recover from the *Daily Mail* libel case and its aftermath. As expected, various pressures were exerted on the government by some Members of Parliament, the media, as well as sections of the public. These pressures were directed mostly to areas such as restricting the cult's activities and ending its privileged charitable status.

Certainly in the United States, the influence of the Moonies has grown considerably over the past twenty years. One disturbing development was his establishing of the *Washington Times* in 1982. On the fifteenth anniversary of its establishment, Rev. Moon delivered a major address to guests and the paper's staff. Amongst many other things, he referred to 1975-76 when the Moonies 'moved into New York City and bought the New Yorker Hotel to serve as its World Mission Center, paying only 5.6 million dollars'. Referring to the *Washington Times*, he acknowledged that 'literally, nine hundred million to one billion dollars has been spent to activate and run' the paper.

He then boasted of the paper's enormous influence on some American presidents, including Reagan, and even different government departments. Indeed, he claims that since the time of Ronald Reagan, Rev. Moon — known to his followers as 'Father' — 'has had influence over choosing the right president and Christianity has come to stand more and more on Father's side'.

An exaggeration? Certainly. But do not dismiss this cult as an innocuous, powerless group of idiots. The Moonies have vast sums of money at their disposal and they now own extensive, rich properties as well as many lucrative companies worldwide.

The influence of Rev. Moon, sadly, has grown in recent years and, like an octopus, he has spread his tentacles out into most areas of society in our global village. As illustrated in chapter 4, the cult has poured millions of dollars into Brazil's Pantanal region in an attempt to create an earthly paradise. And in Paraguay, for example, it has acquired over 300,000 hectares of land, which includes the town of Puerto Casado.

The message is loud and clear. Moonies are a force to be reckoned with and they need to be evangelized.

A personal testimony

On a more personal note, a book was published in which the author, Jacqui Williams, describes her four years with the Moonies.[4] It is a sad and frightening story of a young Christian teacher from England who was drawn unknowingly into the web of the Unification Church while on holiday in San Francisco. Impressed by the friendliness and sincerity of her new Moonie friends, Jacqui was oblivious to the brainwashing techniques that were used to make her a follower of Rev. Moon. She then spent much of her time fund-raising for the cult, but after four years she had to return unexpectedly to England. Jacqui did not like what she saw of the Moonies in England and she left their headquarters to return to her family. Very slowly, she was helped by family and friends to renounce the teaching and lifestyle of the Moonies. Reflecting on her experience, she acknowledges that she was deceived, but in a subtle way, and she now wants to warn others of the dangers.

'They are desperate', insists Jacqui, 'to gain recognition from the Christian church, and they are now more likely to join local churches and work from inside them.' Her message to us is loud and clear: if Christians are to weaken the influence of Moonies then people must be given information and teaching. But that is not all. Love and concern must be shown to those caught in the web of this evil cult.

RELEVANT COMPARISONS

The Unification Church	The Bible
GOD	
God is an invisible essence manifesting the qualities of spirit and energy from which all that exists is generated. 'God is living in me and I am the incarnation of himself. The whole world is in my hand and I will conquer and subjugate the world' (Rev. Sun Myung Moon).	'The LORD reigns' (Psalm 97:1). 'All the peoples of the earth are regarded as nothing. He does as he pleases with the powers of heaven and the peoples of the earth' (Daniel 4:35; cf. Jeremiah 10:10). 'God is spirit' (John 4:24). 'Now to the King eternal, immortal, invisible, the only God, be honour and glory for ever and ever' (1 Timothy 1:17).
BIBLE	
'Until our mission with the Christian church is over, we must quote the Bible and use it to explain the *Divine Principle*. After we receive the inheritance of the Christians, we will be free to teach without the Bible' (Rev. Sun Myung Moon in Master Speaks, March-April 1965).	'Heaven and earth will pass away, but my words will never pass away' (Luke 21:33). 'Your word is truth' (John 17:17).

PERSON OF CHRIST

The only difference between Jesus and other men was the fact that he had no original sin. Rev. Moon stands above all previous saints, prophets and religious leaders and is greater than Jesus Christ himself.

'No heroes in the past, no saints or holy men in the past, like Jesus, or Confucius, have excelled us' (Rev. Sun Myung Moon).

'No one has ever seen God, but God, the One and Only, who is at the Father's side, has made him known' (John 1:18).

'I am the way and the truth and the life. No one comes to the Father, except through me' (John 14:6).

DEATH OF CHRIST

The mission of Jesus in the world was to take a bride in the place of Eve, marry and produce perfect children. By this example, other perfect families would be established and the world perfected.

But Jesus failed because he was crucified before he could marry. It was not God's purpose for him to die. John the Baptist's failure was a major cause of the crucifixion. God allowed Satan to invade the physical body of Jesus and crucify him.

'The LORD has laid on him the iniquity of us all' (Isaiah 53:6).

'For the Son of Man came to seek and to save what was lost' (Luke 19:10).

'Christ Jesus came into the world to save sinners' (1 Timothy 1:15).

'But when this priest had offered for all time one sacrifice for sins, he sat down at the right hand of God' (Hebrews 10:12; cf. Acts 2:23).

RESURRECTION OF CHRIST

Jesus was raised as a spirit-man from the dead and in this way redeemed man spiritually.

'"Destroy this temple, and I will raise it again in three days"... But the temple he had spoken of was his body' (John 2:19-21; cf. 1 John 3:2-3).

HOLY SPIRIT

The Holy Spirit is female and has been one of the true parents of humanity with Jesus.

'If I go, I will send him to you' (John 16:7).

SECOND COMING

Jesus himself will not return. The Lord of the Second Advent will be born in Korea as the King of kings. Rev. Moon is this Lord and has been confirmed as such throughout the spirit world. He now provides additional revelation.

1960 (the year that Rev. Moon married Hak Ja Han) saw the dawning of a new age when the marriage of the Lamb foretold in Revelation 19 took place. The Lord of the Second Advent and his bride became the true parents of mankind. In the 1980s or from then onwards this new messiah will be revealed to the world.

'...if anyone says to you, "Look, here is the Christ!"; or, "Look, there he is!" do not believe it. For false Christs and false prophets will appear' (Mark 13:21-22).

'Be on guard! Be alert! You do not know when that time will come' (Mark 13:33).

'This same Jesus, who has been taken from you into heaven, will come back in the same way you have seen him go into heaven' (Acts 1:11).

'...as you eagerly wait for our Lord Jesus Christ to be revealed' (1 Corinthians 1:7).

'...and to wait for his Son from heaven, whom he raised from the dead — Jesus, who rescues us from the coming wrath' (1 Thessalonians 1:10).

FUTURE STATE

Everyone will be saved eventually. When Rev. Moon as messiah reveals himself to the world, the spirits of those who have died will join Moon's followers so they can develop into divine spirits. Reincarnation also applies to evil people. Through science the earth will be restored, then all the religions of the world will be unified.

'This is how it will be at the end of the age. The angels will come and separate the wicked from the righteous and throw them into the fiery furnace' (Matthew 13:49-50).

'...for whom blackest darkness has been reserved for ever' (Jude 13).

'If anyone's name was not found written in the book of life, he was thrown into the lake of fire' (Revelation 20:15).

CREATION

Creation is the body or outward form of God, so everything is ultimately part of the substance called God.

'By the word of the LORD were the heavens made' (Psalm 33:6).

'It is I who made the earth and created mankind upon it. My own hands stretched out the heavens; I marshalled their starry hosts' (Isaiah 45:12).

'By faith we understand that the universe was formed at God's command' (Hebrews 11:3).

MAN

From out of himself, God projected spirit beings. When a spirit is born into a body here it then becomes a form spirit. Each person has a physical man and a spiritual man. The first two

Although created in the image of God (Genesis 1:26-27), man remains only a creature and is distinct from God the Creator.

'The God who made the world and everything in it is

persons, Adam and Eve, like every other person since, were a special part of God's infinite nature.

the Lord of heaven and earth' (Acts 17:24; cf. Isaiah 42:5; Psalms 102:25-27; 90:2).

SIN

Before Adam and Eve could achieve perfection (i.e. marriage and the forming of a trinity with God, thus producing children free of sin), Eve fornicated with Lucifer, with the result that mankind fell spiritually.

In a vain attempt to repair this damage, Eve persuaded Adam to live with her as husband, but he had not attained perfection either, so this union caused the physical fall of mankind. Eve and then Adam received the sinful features of Lucifer.

Sin is not fornication with Lucifer, but transgression of the law (1 John 3:4). This sin affected the whole subsequent history of mankind.

'...just as sin entered the world through one man, and death through sin, and in this way death came to all men, because all sinned' (Romans 5:12).

THE GUIDE

CHAPTER SEVENTEEN

THE FAMILY OF LOVE

A BRIEF HISTORY

This cult was described by the *Daily Telegraph* (24 March 2000) as 'a British-based sex cult', which caused problems in East Africa when the Kenyan government officials placed all government-run schools and children's homes on alert. The reason? Members of the 'Family of Love' were believed to be actively recruiting members in Uganda and Kenya.

Children's homes

Sammy Kwallah, director of children's services in Kenya's Home Ministry, explained that an unexpected visit by two suspected members of 'The Family' had been made to a Barnardo's home in the Nairobi suburb of Langata. They may also have visited other children's homes.

While there is no firm evidence of any abuse, Mr Kwallah explained that 'their motives are highly suspect. Their target is children in Kenyan institutions.' The British High Commission in Kenya announced that it contacted the Kenyan government concerning the possibility that cult members were active in the country.

Was the Kenyan government official overreacting? Many observers agreed that the official acted responsibly and that children are indeed at risk from members of the Family of Love. One UK source[1] claimed that 'it is difficult to find a cult with a worse reputation'. In October 1994, for example, a teenage girl received £5,000 from the British Criminal Injuries Compensation Board for having been abused from the age of three by members of this cult.

Of nearly twelve thousand current members of the Family of Love, it is estimated that two-thirds are children. These are the result of the cult's 'Hookers for Christ' campaign in the 1970s and 1980s, in which female members seduced potential converts and bore their children.

As communal living became a prominent feature of the cult, members 'shared' wives and husbands, sex with children was condoned, and immoral practices were used by women members to attract men to the cult.

History

How did this cult begin? The cult's own web site traces its origins to 1968 and Huntingdon Beach, California, where David Berg and his wife commenced 'a ministry to the counter culture youth who flocked to that seaside town'.

Berg's parents were active Christians, and his father was an evangelist working with the Christian and

Missionary Alliance in the United States. Berg himself had felt God's call to preach, and eventually he served as pastor of an Alliance church in Arizona. Then, for a brief period, he assisted a Pentecostal pastor in radio work until he moved to Huntingdon Beach with his family.

Here, Berg was involved in evangelizing young people and was responsible for coffee-bar work. Increasingly he became part of the 'Jesus Movement' with its characteristics of intensive evangelism (employing new and questionable methods), community living, authoritarian leadership, and the criticism and rejection of other churches.

Berg's group emerged as a strong and popular subdivision of the Jesus Movement in the late 1970s.

Teens for Christ

At this time, Berg established an organization called 'Teens for Christ'. Converts were encouraged to leave their homes, jobs and churches, to settle into one of his many communal groups.

Berg tended to attract restless and alienated young people from the middle class. It was a journalist who, in 1969, renamed the early members as 'The Children of God'. As these young members travelled to different American states, so the movement gained momentum and quickly spread overseas.

By 1972 they had 130 communities scattered throughout the world. Six years later in 1978, the cult was formally dissolved and a new group, now called The Family of Love, was established with a different organizational structure. Today, the cult is more often referred to simply as The Family. Their founder and leader, David Brandt Berg, died in 1994 at the age of seventy-five.

Numbers

How strong is this cult today? Their official answer is that there are 'approximately 12,000 full-time and associate adult' members working in 'over 1400 centres or communities, situated in over 100 countries'.

These members are drawn from more than ninety nationalities 'and when possible are joined in their ministries by their children'. And how successful have they been? They inform us that they have shared the gospel message 'with over 237 million individuals, while billions have heard' it through the mass media.

Their further claim is that 'over 23.3 million people have personally prayed with our members to receive God's love, forgiveness and salvation'. In addition, 850 million pieces of gospel literature have been distributed in sixty-one languages and eight million audio tapes in more than twenty languages have also been given away.

Caution needed

One must be cynical with regard to some of these official statistics. For example, they wrongly assume that the 23 million who made professions of faith with their workers were actually converted. What is important is an inward, supernatural and radical work of new birth by the Holy Spirit in the individual. Sadly, some of those who profess faith in the Lord Jesus do so without this prior, divine work of new birth having taken place.

Anyway, if so many people had prayed with their members and received forgiveness, why is their membership only 12,000? The statistics must clearly be treated with considerable caution.

However, even after making appropriate allowances, these statistics do highlight the influence which the cult still exercises in many countries. 1400 communities in over 100 countries, together with the distribution of 850 million pieces of literature and eight million audio tapes must have made a significant impact on many individuals. And this should concern us deeply.

Methods

What methods do they use for recruiting members? In addition to publications, audio/video tapes and their web site, their members 'also regularly perform at musical benefits' and are involved in humanitarian work.

They also 'minister' in nightclubs where young people predominate, and use musical groups and street theatre in an attempt to win converts. Over the years, many of their methods have been criticized as being unbiblical and even immoral. In fact, Berg's writings were often pornographic in content and obsessed with sex. Women members were instructed to 'crucify the flesh' by giving themselves physically to men in order to attract them to the cult and to Christ. This was regarded as an expression of God's love which, according to Berg, is only properly experienced in sexual intercourse.

Such methods are far removed from those taught and used in the New Testament. The apostle Paul could say of his evangelism: 'You are witnesses, and so is God, of how holy, righteous and blameless we were among you…' (1 Thessalonians 2:10; 4:7). Our holy, sin-hating God does not allow his people to use immoral behaviour, not even for purposes of evangelism.

Beliefs

'The Family' sets out, carefully and in detail, its 'fundamental beliefs and essential doctrines'. In general theological terms, the cult is Arminian, charismatic, pre-millennialist and separatist. To be fair, however, there are positive features in their doctrinal statement. For example, they are Trinitarian and hold strongly to the deity of Christ. Salvation, too, 'is wholly by grace' through the 'substitutionary sacrifice and death of the Just for the unjust'. It is appropriated by personal faith in Jesus Christ, and 'Once saved, the believer shall be kept saved for ever' by God's power. These emphases are welcomed.

What then is wrong with this cult? The major problem here is common to a number of other cults, namely, inconsistency. While this cult acknowledges the Bible's supreme authority, in practice Berg's writings are given greater prominence.

After Berg withdrew in the early 1970s from daily involvement in the group's activities, he became known as 'Moses' and communicated with followers through his 'MO letters', many of which were published. He claimed that the Bible is God's 'inspired word for yesterday' but the 'Moses letters' are God's inspired word for today and the only valid interpretation of the Bible.

That is gross error, for 'the word of the Lord stands for ever' (1 Peter 1:25). Quite often Berg's 'teachings are but rules taught by men' and 'nullify the word of God…' (Mark 7:7, 13).

Questions

Imagine the scene: a young Christian is surfing the Internet. He is eager to visit as many Christian web sites as possible. His purpose? To be more aware of what the Lord is doing through Christians.

He also wants to discover some helpful resources for learning more about the Bible. Quite early on he visits The Family of Love's web site. Impressed by their emphasis on doctrine, he downloads the thirteen pages containing the cult's 'Essential doctrines'. He is excited and reads them carefully.

There are questions in his mind as he reads. Do they believe in the Trinity? What about Christ's deity, virgin birth, sinlessness and unique death on the cross? Are they right about sin?

Reassured

He is reassured and it gets even better when he reads their statement on 'The Way of Salvation'. John 3:16 is prominent on this web page: 'For God so loved the world that He gave His only begotten Son, that whoever believes in Him should not perish but have everlasting life.' And the explanation of this key verse further encourages him: 'All persons who personally accept God's pardon for sin through Jesus Christ will be forgiven.' Jesus is the 'sacrificial lamb who alone can take away our sins' through his 'substitutionary sacrifice and death of the Just for the unjust'.

These statements express the heart of the biblical gospel. There was more to encourage this Internet user. He reads that believers are 'saved for ever', indwelt by the Holy Spirit, and 'enjoy sweet, intimate personal communion with the Lord'.

However, encouragement then begins to give way to feelings of unease concerning some of the twenty-eight doctrines detailed on this web site.

Dangers

An imaginary situation? Not really. But why mention it here? There are several reasons for doing so. Firstly, the Internet is an invaluable and rich resource; yet it is fraught with dangers. And the reason is simple. The Internet provides access to a wide spectrum of beliefs and morals ranging from pornographic, occult, cult and gay propaganda to useful educational data and edifying Christian material.

Unknowingly, this young Christian had wandered on to a cult web site. Surfers need to be cautious.

Secondly, this Christian surfer soon began to realize that in the hands of some people, truth can be mixed with error. He is to be commended for making a quick exit from The Family web site. And what he did next was even better. He turned to his Bible and checked their teachings by this divine, absolute standard.

Interpretations

What was troubling him? I want to mention two of his concerns. Statement 12 entitled 'Spirits of Departed Saints' was a major problem for him and rightly so. He read: 'God on occasions also uses the spirits of departed saints to minister and deliver messages to His people.' For 'scriptural evidence' they misuse three Bible references.

The first is to 'the appearance of the departed prophet Samuel's spirit to king Saul' (1 Samuel 28), a favourite argument of other cults like Spiritism. Two different answers have been given by Christians in interpreting the incident. Some suggest the séance was faked by the witch, because God alone has power over the dead and he forbids contact between the dead and the living. God would not have given another revelation, least of all in a way forbidden in the Bible, after having already rejected the king for his disobedience. It is interesting that it was Saul who ordered the witch to contact Samuel.

The woman could have faked it all, describing Samuel (v. 14) in the way that she herself remembered the prophet in his lifetime. It is a plausible explanation especially as the text itself makes it clear that Saul did not himself see Samuel.

Only through Scripture

However, the words delivered to Saul are an authentic (though damning) prophecy. An alternative explanation, therefore, is that God did permit Samuel to speak, but not in response to the witch. Rather, God brought it about in order to punish Saul further.

Samuel did not return at the request of the medium but at God's command in order to declare a final message of doom upon Saul. In other words, this is strictly an isolated incident. God's revealed will forbids, and condemns, any contact with spirits or the dead (see, e.g. Deuteronomy 18:10-11; Isaiah 8:19-20).

Contrary to what The Family claims, God does not 'minister ... to His people' through those who have died. It is only through the Bible that he speaks to us.

Moses and Elijah

What about 'the departed prophets, Moses and Elijah, appearing and conferring with Jesus'? Does this support their claim? Again the answer is 'no'.

The transfiguration of Jesus Christ was a unique moment in salvation-history. It prepared the Lord Jesus to face his approaching suffering and death and also strengthened the faith of Peter, James and John (Matthew 17:1-8), deepening their awareness of Christ's glory.

That 'Moses and Elijah appeared' (v. 3) there is no dispute. How the disciples were able to recognize them, we do not know. But why should only Moses and Elijah appear? The answer is that these two outstanding Old Testament characters represent, respectively, the Law and the Prophets. In the transfiguration, both pointed to Jesus Christ as God, the one who fulfils the Old Testament and died uniquely for sinners.

Did God use Moses and Elijah (as The Family believe) to 'deliver messages' to the disciples? Certainly not. Notice that these heavenly visitors did not speak to Peter, James and John at all; they were only 'talking with Jesus' (v. 3). Also observe that the disciples did not attempt to speak to Moses and Elijah. When Peter spoke, it was to Jesus only.

Healing from the cross?

A second concern of the young Christian relates to the death of Jesus. Yes, the Lord 'gave himself as the only ransom for sinners'. That is gloriously true. But, he asks, is it correct that Jesus died to save us not only from sin, but also from disease? Having also heard charismatic friends teaching this idea, just like The Family (Statement 16), he is eager to find out what the Bible says.

When he checks, he realizes that Isaiah 53 is an important chapter. The reason? Because verses 4 and 5 from that chapter are used in turn in Matthew 8:17 and 1 Peter 2:24.

In the first reference Matthew writes: 'This was to fulfil what was spoken through the prophet Isaiah, "He took up our infirmities and carried our diseases".'

Matthew here relates Isaiah's words to the Lord's healing and exorcising ministry described in verses 1-16 of chapter 8.

Does Isaiah 53:4, therefore, speak of Christ's healing ministry on earth before referring to his sufferings in the rest of the verse? This is possible. If so, the reference is to just that: the unique ministry of healing carried out by Jesus to authenticate him as the Messiah (Luke 4:18-21; John 14:11). It cannot be pressed further to imply that every Christian has the right to physical healing. Indeed, this would contradict the clear teaching of other Scriptures (e.g. 2 Corinthians 12:7-10).

Spiritual healing

However, the word 'sickness' used by Isaiah may only be a picture to describe sin. 1 Peter 2:24 makes it clear that physical healing is not in view. The context only has the spiritual condition of people in mind, for the words 'by his wounds you have been healed' are appended to the statement that believers might 'die to sins' and 'live for righteousness'.

In any case, Isaiah 53:5, which Peter quotes, itself provides the reason for Christ's sufferings on the cross: 'He was pierced for our transgressions, he was crushed for our iniquities' and 'for the transgression of my people he was stricken' (Isaiah 53:8). The benefits for us of Christ's sufferings follow, namely, peace with God and spiritual healing.

Tired but happier, my young Christian friend retired to bed after e-mailing his church pastor to share what he had studied that evening. He is convinced that the cross is about sin, forgiveness and a right relationship with God. It is not even partly about healing. He is right.

RELEVANT COMPARISONS

The Family of Love	The Bible
BIBLE	
1. The Bible is God's 'inspired word for yesterday', while the 'Moses letters' (MO letters are those written by David Berg, who later adopted the name Moses David) are the inspired word of God for today.	1. 'Your word, O LORD, is eternal; it stands firm in the heavens' (Psalm 119:89). 'All your words are true; all your righteous laws are eternal' (Psalm 119:160).
2. The MO letters are more authoritative than the Bible and are the only valid interpretation of the Bible. Berg is regarded as God's 'mouthpiece', through whom alone the correct understanding of the Scripture has been given.	2. '...their teachings are but rules taught by men' (Mark 7:7). 'Thus you nullify the word of God by your tradition that you have handed down' (Mark 7:13).

SALVATION

Conventional churches belong to the devil. Berg writes, 'We teach the kids to hate ... the false church system... We hate the hypocrisy, self-righteousness, lies and deceitfulness of those who claim to be the Church, but are not and we hate the spiritual system of the Devil behind them.'

While many conventional churches have abandoned Bible doctrine and ethics yet the true church of God is visible in the world; it consists of all those who trust in Christ and have been born of the Holy Spirit (1 Corinthians 1:2; 1 Peter 1:1-2).

DISCIPLESHIP

Misusing our Lord's words in Matthew 10:34-37, Berg taught that following Christ necessitates the forsaking of families, friends and employment, etc. and this wrong teaching has had tragic results for many families.

In Matthew 10:34-37 the Lord is stressing the believer's supreme loyalty to Christ. The gospel of Christ divides as well as unites families, for man's sinful nature frequently causes him to ridicule the gospel (1 Corinthians 1:23; 2:14) and oppose even relatives who become Christians. There are occasions, then, when Christ must come before parents and others but, wherever possible, the law of God insists that children should honour their parents (see Exodus 20:12; Ephesians 6:1-3). Berg's interpretation of Ephesians 6:1-2, namely, that obeying parents means obeying your spiritual, not human, parents is a perverse twisting of these verses. The word can only refer to human parents and children must honour them as far as is possible, for this is what the Lord demands.

The Family of Love also exploits members by taking all their money and worldly goods.

'You know we never used flattery, nor did we put on a mask to cover up greed — God is our witness' (1 Thessalonians 2:5).

'...they are ruining whole households by teaching things they ought not to teach — and that for the sake of dishonest gain' (Titus 1:11; cf. 1 Timothy 6:3-16).

MARRIAGE AND SEX

1. Abraham, Solomon and David had concubines so Berg insists it is legitimate to have sex with others in the group.

1. The marriage of a man and a woman is an ordinance of God (Genesis 2:18-24); sex is God's gift to be used exclusively within the marriage relationship. The lapses of even godly men must not be taken as God's norm for mankind. These were departures from the original creation ordinance of marriage and were associated with backsliding (e.g. Solomon), unbelief, sin and trouble as in the cases of Abraham (Genesis 21), David (2 Samuel 11, 13) and Hannah (1 Samuel 1:1-6).

COMPARISONS

2. Husband and wife-swapping is justified by a wrong interpretation of Acts 2:44.

2. The sharing of 'everything in common' (Acts 2:44) is explained in verse 45 as being applicable only to possessions and material goods. This extensive sharing of goods was not a regular practice for the imperfect tenses are used by Luke, e.g. 'they used to sell' and 'they gave'.

3. Berg's writings are often pornographic and obsessed with sex. Women members are told to 'crucify the flesh' by giving themselves physically to other men in order to attract them to the group and to Christ. This is an expression of God's love which, Berg claims, is only properly experienced in sexual intercourse.

3. See 1 Corinthians 6:12-20; 7:1-40; 2 Corinthians 7:1; Ephesians 5:3-17; Colossians 3:5-8; 1 Thessalonians 4:3-8.

OCCULT

Occult practices such as astrology and witchcraft are encouraged in the MO letters. Berg himself claimed to be led by a spirit identified as a gypsy king who died over a thousand years ago; Berg also claimed regular demonic intercourse.

Deuteronomy 18:10-12; Isaiah 8:19-22.

SECOND COMING OF CHRIST

Their earlier prediction that Jesus would return to earth in 1993 was proved wrong.

'No one knows about that day or hour, not even the angels in heaven, nor the Son, but only the Father' (Matthew 24:36, 42, 44).

CHAPTER EIGHTEEN

SCIENTOLOGY

A BRIEF HISTORY

'The fastest growing religious movement on earth...' That is what the Scientology organization claims for itself.[1] It is a staggering claim to make and there is no firm evidence to substantiate it, particularly in comparison with all the other religious movements operating worldwide.

Their official web site reports that 'Scientology is practised in more than 125 countries.'[2] The official web page claims 'there are more than 3,200 churches, missions and groups in 154 countries'.[3] The discrepancy in the number of countries may be due to the fact that in a few of the 154 countries, Scientology is not yet being 'practised'. In Great Britain they claim a membership of about half a million, and several churches.

The web sites quoted above make the further claim that 'Scientology has become a firmly established and active force for positive change in the world in less than half a century.' In a word, it boasts that 'Scientology works'.

And the evidence? Well, they inform us that 'millions of people the world over use its principles in their daily lives' and also 'a growing number of people find relevance in Scientology for themselves, their families, their organizations, their nations and this entire civilization'.

An exaggeration? Yes because there are many disillusioned ex-members of this organization who question their beliefs, methods of recruitment and the claims made for the cult's teaching and success. But we will return to the point later.

The aims of Scientology were articulated clearly by their founder, L. Ron Hubbard: 'A civilization without insanity, without criminals and without war, where the able can prosper and honest beings can have rights, and where man is free to rise to greater heights, are the aims of Scientology.'

These aims sound fantastic but they are unattainable on the basis of the Scientology creed. For one thing, their view of human nature is superficial, optimistic and unbiblical. They hold that humans are inherently good; anti-social and unreasonable behaviour are attributed to a highly dubious and far-fetched theory of 'engrams' (psychological difficulties). But the Bible teaches that it is sin, not 'engrams', which has invaded, twisted and controlled all of our human lives. And, as we will see, only Christ can recreate and rebuild human lives in a radically different way leading to real and lasting harmony, peace and, ultimately in heaven, a perfect but redeemed humanity. Therefore, do not be deceived by the aims of Scientology for they are wholly unrealistic.

I acknowledge that this organization seeks to provide practical help for people in needy areas of the world.

For example, one of their official web pages covers the story of their 'Volunteer Ministers' continuing to provide aid in the early months of 2005 for the victims of the Tsunami disaster in South-East Asia. 'Based on the belief that you cannot free yourself spiritually without working to free others',[4] 'Scientology has founded and supports many organizations for social betterment, particularly in the areas of drug abuse, crime, psychiatric abuse, government abuse of law, human rights, religious freedom, education and morality.' But as you might expect, 'Scientology strongly favours the use of their methodology for spiritual/mental healing over the use of conventional treatment.'

Their official web site reports that, 'A person discovering Scientology for the first time usually reads a book, learns about the subject from a friend, attends a lecture in someone's home or takes an introductory course…'[5]

Those who share the Scientology message with others are called 'field auditors' and then there are 'groups and missions of Scientology, which exist to minister the religion at the grassroots level'. At a higher level are the 'more established churches of Scientology which are the centres for Scientology in their cities and the focal points for many community outreach activities'. Then there are 'the more advanced Scientology churches' which 'minister the highest levels of auditing and training…'

The worldwide churches of Scientology are 'organized in a hierarchical structure' and the whole organization is vast and complex. In fact, the title 'Church of Scientology' is a misnomer for, writes Tory Christman, 'in reality, global Scientology is a complex international legal structure of multi-corporations, some of which are non-profit and some of which are not'.[6]

The historical background

Where did this movement begin? When? Well, L. Ron Hubbard was the founder. Hubbard, the son of an American naval commander, was born in Nebraska, USA, in 1911. As his father's work involved constant travel, Hubbard spent his early childhood years with his grandfather, but he was later allowed to join his parents in the Far East. Here the young Hubbard was fascinated by Asian religions and he became absorbed in the study of man himself. After extensive travel in the following years, he pursued and failed a college course in molecular and atomic physics before turning in the 1930s to writing for his livelihood.

During the Second World War he served in the United States navy but there are conflicting accounts of this period in his life. The 'official' Scientology story is that Hubbard was a nuclear physicist but was eventually wounded in action with the navy and taken 'crippled and blinded' to a naval hospital where within two years he claims to have achieved fitness again due to his discovery of 'Dianetics' and Scientology.

The real story, however, is somewhat different. There is no evidence of his being wounded or being involved in combat during the last war but he was discharged from the navy and given a 40% disability pension on the ground of his arthritis and ulcer complaints. He was also given psychiatric treatment because of his suicidal tendencies and depression.

In 1949 Hubbard attributed an improvement in health to his discovery of 'Dianetics' and a year later he published his first book entitled *Dianetics: The Modern Science of Mental Health*, which dealt psychologically with the 'reactive' or subconscious mind. From this inauspicious beginning, Scientology developed and now claims a world membership of fifteen million. The full title of the group is the Church of Scientology and its aim is 'to establish a religious fellowship and association for the research into the spirit and human souls, and the use and dissemination of its findings'.

Ronald E. de Wolf is the oldest of Hubbard's seven children and helped his father establish the Church of Scientology in 1952. In 1959, however, he left the organization, thoroughly disillusioned as his father had become 'further and further removed from reality', suffering from severe paranoia and delusion, and physical ill-health. 'In the process of trying to unravel Scientology out of my head,' he claimed, 'I read the Bible, and in the course of time became a Christian.'[7]

Hubbard's son regards the Scientology church as a sham. 'My father', he says, 'claimed that his theories relating to Scientology were based on thirty years of case histories and research. In fact, they were written off the top of his head while he was under the influence of drugs.'[8]

The Church of Scientology reported Hubbard's death on 25 January 1986 at his ranch in California at the age of seventy-four. In the obituary notice, *The Times* concluded: 'Hubbard was the Henry Ford of occultism. He was not, by any standards, a nice man, but was a highly influential figure among the myriad inventors of magical and religious systems who have appeared in modern times.'[9]

Almost a month later, British friends and devotees of Hubbard paid for a full-page advertisement in the *Daily Telegraph* as a tribute to their leader. They described him as 'best-selling author ... founder of Scientology ... friend to millions'.[10]

Hubbard wrote 'scores of books, more than 15,000 pages of technical writing' and over 3000 of his lectures are available on tape. He claims to have 'discovered a workable means to set men spiritually free — to replace ignorance with knowledge, doubts with certainty and misery with happiness'.[11]

But is Scientology a religion? Well, that is what it claims on the above web page. And one 'prime', 'fundamental' truth it embraces is that 'man is a spiritual being endowed with abilities well beyond those which he normally envisages'. It is Scientology, we are informed, which is able to offer spiritual freedom. In fact, they tell us, 'Scientology is an applied religious philosophy';[12] in other words, not only is it practical but, they insist, it is also a religion that works.

However, a growing number of people disagree and are extremely critical of most, if not all, aspects of Scientology. For example, there are now many ex-members of the cult as well as many web sites where some of these people relate their experiences in Scientology and their reasons for leaving. Videos are also available at *http://www.xenuty.com* in which people who did most or all of the 'Bridge' are speaking out (i. e. those who have completed a number of courses and are well into the cult). One former member explains he was 'in great standing' in the cult for thirty years. He reports that 'many have been lied to, betrayed, abused, deceived. These are common denominators for people who woke up finally...'

This same web site, not unexpectedly, claims that Scientology 'is a vicious and dangerous cult that masquerades as a religion. Its purpose is to make money. It practices a variety of mind-control techniques on people lured into its midst to gain control over their money and their lives...'[13] It is strong language but such critics are prepared to support their statements with reference to their own experiences or other facts.

1995 is often regarded 'as the year the battle between Scientology and its critics on the Internet became a full-scale war, with battles being fought in the real world as well as online'.[14] The organization has set up its own web pages and attempted to answer its critics. Its pages contain only positive references to Scientology and completely omit important information given in the affidavits; no mention is made of the newsgroup *alt.religion.scientology*. Recently, the Google search engine refused to accept advertisements critical of Scientology and this decision has led to a great deal of friction.

The Scientology movement has been plagued by extensive and recurring criticism and allegations since the 1960s. A number of high profile lawsuits in the United States in the 1970s and 1980s resulted in the prosecution of some members or damages being awarded to 'victims'. In Britain, lawsuits in the same period involving Scientology led to a government ban being imposed on all overseas members of the movement who wanted to study or work at British Scientology centres.

It is reasonable to claim that 'Scientology has earned a reputation for itself as one of the most litigious organizations in history; it has filed hundreds of lawsuits (some say thousands) against a considerable number of its critics and opponents through the years, and it has procured an amazing record of legal costs. Scientology has spent millions of dollars over the years in its attacks on its enemies.'[15]

Sadly, Hubbard's writings continue to deceive millions of people and 'The god of this age has blinded the minds of unbelievers, so that they cannot see the light of the gospel of the glory of Christ, who is the image of God' (2 Corinthians 4:4).

It is now time to examine the teaching of Scientology in the light of the Bible and to highlight some of the main errors of this strange movement.

RELEVANT COMPARISONS

Scientology	The Bible
GOD	
While Hubbard believed in the existence of God, there is no official or orthodox doctrine of God in his writings. God is assumed to be impersonal but divine holiness is ignored. Individual members are free to believe what they like about the character and purposes of God. In fact, whether people believe in a God or a plurality of gods or even no god is 'something personal'[16] and therefore Scientology 'offers no specific dogma. The nature of the Supreme Being is revealed personally through each individual as s/he becomes more conscious and spiritually aware.	'In the past God spoke to our forefathers through the prophets at many times and in various ways, but in these last days he has spoken to us by his Son...' (Hebrews 1:1-2). 'Holy, Holy, Holy, is the LORD Almighty; the whole earth is full of his glory' (Isaiah 6:3).

There exists a life energy or force (Theta) beyond and within all'.

BIBLE

The Bible is only one of the numerous 'holy' books; its teaching, therefore, is not binding upon people. The Bible is viewed as one account of people's search after truth. Hubbard himself and his writings are the group's supreme authority.

'Your word is truth' (John 17:17).

'Your word, O LORD, is eternal; it stands firm in the heavens' (Psalm 119:89).

CHRIST

Christ is unimportant in this cult and there are very few references to Christ in their publications. Jesus Christ is respected as one of the great religious teachers.

However, they refuse to accept the possibility of a unique, human incarnation of God. Their reason is that Theta, the universal life force, abides in all. Each human is an immortal spiritual being (thetan) and has the potential of reaching almost a godlike state if the instructions and techniques of Scientology are followed.

'You are the Christ, the Son of the living God' (Matthew 16:16).

'This is my Son, whom I love; with him I am well pleased' (Matthew 17:5).

'He is the image of the invisible God... For by him all things were created ... He is before all things, and in him all things hold together. And he is the head of the body, the church ... so that in everything he might have the supremacy' (Colossians 1:15-18).

'...many false prophets have gone out into the world. This is how you can recognize the Spirit of God: Every spirit that acknowledges that Jesus Christ has come in the flesh is from God, but every spirit that does not acknowledge Jesus is not from God...' (1 John 4:1-3).

MAN

Human beings willed themselves into existence trillions of years ago and then proceeded to will the material universe into being. In doing this, humans were trapped in physical bodies and they need to be 'untrapped' in order to return to their original god-like state. This requires the help of Scientology 'ministers', who can charge over $300 an hour. Human nature is basically good and evil is merely unreasonable or irrational behaviour caused by 'engrams'.

'There is no one righteous, not even one' (Romans 3:10).

'I know that nothing good lives in me, that is, in my sinful nature' (Romans 7:18).

SALVATION

Psychological difficulties (what Hubbard calls 'engrams') spoil man's good nature. Salvation is obtained through the cult's philosophy and methods (i.e. sharing, counselling, confession, etc.) as

'For it is by grace you have been saved, through faith — and this not from yourselves, it is the gift of God — not by works, so that no one can boast' (Ephesians 2:8-9).

'Salvation is found in no

individuals achieve for themselves fulfilment and release.

Fulfilment is realizing one's true nature as an immortal spirit, a thetan. The path to salvation or enlightenment involves attaining conditions of greater mental awareness known as Pre-Clear, Clear and then Operating Thetan. The latter is a spirit capable of controlling matter, energy, time, space, thought and life. Their counsellors (called 'Auditors' or practitioners) help people to recognize their pre-birth, present (called 'auditing') and past disturbances which obstruct the path to spiritual enlightenment and happiness.

one else, for there is no other name under heaven given to men by which we must be saved' (Acts 4:12).

AFTER DEATH

Individuals are reborn continually until the time when they deliberately and consciously face up to all their disturbances and traumas whether in pre-birth or the previous life or the present life. Only then can the spirit escape the monotonous cycle of birth and death then become one with 'God'.

At death, we all enter an eternal destiny in either heaven or hell; our destiny is sealed when we die — there is no escape for unbelievers from hell (see, e.g., Matthew 25:46; Luke 16:23, 25-26; Romans 6:23; 2 Thessalonians 1:8-9; Hebrews 9:27).

THE GUIDE

CHAPTER NINETEEN

FREEMASONRY

A BRIEF HISTORY

Estimates of the worldwide membership of Freemasonry vary from between three and six million, with about 25,000 lodges. But there are over one million members and 9,950 lodges in Great Britain alone. Only men are eligible for membership and they must be over the age of twenty-one, although the sons of Freemasons are allowed to join at the age of eighteen.

In America, the Freemasons are actively and openly recruiting new members. Membership there has fallen from 4.1 million in 1959 to about 1.7 million in 2004 with many members being elderly. One grand master, Daniel Wilson, believes 'there are plenty of men looking for the camaraderie and fraternalism that we provide.'[1]

'If you're looking to make a difference, take a look at Freemasonry', reads the adverts in twelve New Jersey papers. 'We are committed to charity, brotherhood, friendship and faith and do so through philanthropic and humanitarian acts. Become a better man, father, husband and citizen…'

In early 2005 the public response to the recruitment campaign was positive; in Ohio and Pennsylvania it brought in several thousand new members. Women are still not admitted and they must be content to join affiliated organizations.

Despite this new approach in America, the colourful customs and traditions will not be abandoned. The special handshakes, the recitations and the rolled-up left trouser leg are staying.

While clergy from most denominations are involved in Freemasonry, in the United Kingdom, Methodist ministers have their own Epworth Lodge.[2] 'The Church of England', writes Stephen Knight, 'has been a stronghold of Freemasonry for more than 200 years. Traditionally, joining the Brotherhood and advancing within it has always been the key to preferment in the Church. This situation has altered in the past twenty years ... even so, the Church is still rife with members of the Brotherhood.'[3] Some former Archbishops of Canterbury, including Dr Geoffrey Fisher, were Freemasons. Some Anglican bishops also belong to the Brotherhood, as well as many of the lower clergy and laity. Rev. Walter Hannah reports that the SPCK ordered their shops not to stock his book *Darkness Visible*, which was a scathing exposure of Freemasonry.[4] The Archbishop of Canterbury is the SPCK President and the archbishop in office at the time was Dr Geoffrey Fisher!

The Greek Orthodox Church and the Salvation Army, for example, still forbid their people to become Freemasons but the Roman Catholic Church has relaxed its papal edicts of 1738 and 1917 which condemned the group. Since November 1974 any Roman Catholic can join 'if he sincerely believes that membership of Freemasonry does not conflict with his deeper loyalty', but he will be excommunicated 'if the policy and actions of the Freemasons in his area are known to be hostile to the Church'. Stephen Knight claims to have evidence that the Vatican itself is infiltrated by Freemasons.[5] David Yallop also speaks of 'over 100 masons, ranging from cardinals to priests' inside the Vatican and argues convincingly that Pope John Paul I's plan to restrict their influence actually led to his death in 1978.[6]

Numerous members of the Royal Family, too, are Freemasons and the Duke of Kent is the Grand Master of the society. There are reliable reports that the Queen Mother dissuaded Prince Charles from becoming a Freemason and if the prince holds out in his refusal to join, he will be the first king for several generations not to be a mason. His father, Prince Philip, succumbed somewhat reluctantly under the pressure of King George VI, although the prince has not been actively involved in the society and regards much of its ritual as 'a silly joke'.[7]

Those working within industry, commerce and business are frequently involved in Freemasonry, particularly if they want promotion or improved sales. Freemasonry has infiltrated all levels of banking, from clerks to branch/regional/national managerial positions. The Bank of England, for example, has its own lodge and many of its employees are masons.

In most lodges you will find men who are accountants, commercial travellers, architects, shop managers and proprietors, builders, surveyors, estate agents, restaurant proprietors and travel agents, etc. A former master mason writes, 'Membership of Freemasonry is used considerably in the field of industry and commerce — because of the sign one can give which is unnoticeable by anyone else. You can make it known to the other person that you are what they call on the square, and if the other person is on the square he will recognize the sign, and that can influence either your being able to make a sale, or, if you are applying for a job, it can make the difference between whether you get the job or not.'[8]

Another area where Freemasonry is rife is in the legal profession — barristers, magistrates, judges and solicitors. The Law Society, for example, which is the governing body of over 40,000 solicitors in England and Wales, is 'one of the most masonic institutions in the world'.[9] One barrister, Rudy Narayan, claims that out of more than eighty High Court judges in Britain, thirty were Freemasons.[10]

'The insidious effect of Freemasonry among the police has to be experienced to be believed,' claimed the former head of Monmouthshire CID in 1969.[11] Since the Scotland Yard corruption in 1877, followed by the police cover-up of the Jack the Ripper murders in London in 1888 (perpetrated according to masonic ritual), claims of bias towards Freemasonry and its influence within the police force have been made regularly. These claims have been accompanied by some compelling evidence.

In 1984 the Police Federation gave financial support to a Chief Inspector who pressed for an independent enquiry into claims that his career had been unfairly influenced by Freemasonry.[12] Stephen Knight observes that 'Operation Countryman, the biggest investigation ever conducted into police corruption in Britain, would never have come about if the Commissioner of the City of London Police between 1971 and 1977 had not been corrupted and unduly influenced by Freemasonry.'[13] The same writer argues that 'An independent enquiry into Freemasonry in the police should be initiated' immediately. Furthermore, he insists that 'A compulsory register on which police officers have to list their affiliation to secret societies, and their status within such societies, is the minimum requirement if a grave situation is to be improved.'[14]

The historical background

As we have seen, the influence of Freemasonry in our society is extensive; today Freemasonry is the largest international secret society in the world. But how did it begin and where?

Well, it began harmlessly enough. While some masons try to trace their history back to the building of Solomon's temple (in 1 Kings 5), the society really originated in the medieval lodge of the English stonemasons. The main work of these masons was the building of churches and cathedrals, which often involved them in considerable travel. In order to obtain new work it was considered necessary for craft members to keep the skills secret, so various passwords were introduced in order to safeguard these secrets and ensure new work for themselves. The masons also built 'lodges' in close proximity to their work. These were recreational centres where they relaxed and talked together. With the decline of cathedral building, they augmented their numbers with honorary or unskilled members. During the seventeenth century lodges emerged which consisted wholly of unqualified masons. In 1717 all the different lodges united under the Grand Lodge of England and their *Book of Constitutions* was published in 1723.

The *Constitutions*, however, contained major changes which 'de-christianized' the society and authorized the introduction of pagan elements into its ritual. All references to Christ were eliminated and between 1723 and 1813 the invocation of Christ's name at the end of prayers gradually stopped. Even when Scriptures like 1 Peter 2:5 and 2 Thessalonians 3:2, 13 were quoted in masonic ritual the name of Christ was removed from the text. Instead, ancient Egyptian symbolism and ritual of a mystical nature were absorbed into the society in this period to give it a distinctly religious basis and expression. Various splits occurred throughout the eighteenth century, but in 1813 unity was re-established with the formation of the 'United Grand Lodge of Ancient Free and Accepted Masons of England'. While the society has been severely persecuted at times, it has become increasingly more popular and acceptable in Western Europe and North America since the end of World War Two.

A great deal of humanitarian work is undertaken by this society, especially on behalf of its own members. A hospital and nursing home are maintained for sick masons, as well as two schools for the children of masons. There is also a Fund of Benevolence which is used to support needy masons and their dependents. Other charities are also supported by Freemasons but their benevolence falls far below the standard of the New Testament. For example, in the third degree obligation the new member must promise to relieve a brother mason only 'so far as may fairly be done without detriment to myself or my connections'. In America, their charitable work raises more than $750 million a year.

Incompatibility with Christian teaching

There are many features of Freemasonry which are incompatible with the teaching of the Bible and the fact that it is a religion should prevent Christians from participating in its activities. One often hears the comment that masons do not take the religious aspect seriously, but why sing hymns, say prayers, swear oaths on their volume of Sacred Law, or have a temple and altar if this is so?

Another argument raised in defence of Freemasonry is that it is only an arm or extension of the church and not in any sense a rival. But this is unconvincing, for Freemasonry claims to possess secrets which help people to know how to worship and know God better, secrets which the Bible does not reveal and the church does not possess. One such secret is the sacred and mysterious name of God which is found, they claim, only in Freemasonry. The Christian, however, affirms that God has given a sufficient, perfect and final revelation of his character and purpose in the Bible alone. There is no need for additional revelation.

Some masonic writers suggest that initiation to Freemasonry is superior to Christian baptism in that it enriches man's spiritual experience. In this initiation ceremony, the candidate rolls his left trouser leg up to his knee, removes his jacket and tie, opens his shirt, replaces his right shoe with a slipper and empties his pocket of money as a symbol of his poverty. To symbolize 'his state of darkness', the candidate is then blindfolded; he acknowledges that while he is in darkness he is moving into the 'light' which is found supremely in Freemasonry. For the Christian this is offensive. Christ, not Freemasonry, is the light of the world (John 8:12) and only in Christ can we find true, spiritual light. Preaching on the words of 1 Corinthians 3:11 ('For no one can lay any foundation other than the one already laid, which is Jesus Christ'), Rev. A. W.

Rainsbury detailed six Christian objections to Freemasonry.[15]

1. Secret societies are unscriptural (see Matthew 10:26-27; John 18:20).
2. A candidate must make rash promises 'to secrecy and faithfulness in matters of which nothing is revealed to him previously... The man has got to sell his conscience to the Worshipful Master before he can proceed. But what right has any man to make another the custodian of his conscience?' (see Leviticus 5:4-6).
3. The use of monstrous masonic oaths which contradict our Lord's words in Matthew 5:33-37.
4. The exclusion of the Lord Jesus Christ from its precincts. 'The precious name of Jesus Christ is not allowed even to be uttered in a masonic lodge... How can any Christian mason offer such an insult to the One who hung upon the cross to save his precious soul?'
5. It rests upon a false doctrine of justification by works.
6. It is an apostate religion, with its own universal theology which eliminates Jesus Christ. Masons use a pagan, syncretistic name for God — Jah-Bul-On!

'I am firmly convinced,' writes Walter Hannah, 'that for a Christian to pledge himself to a religious or even quasi-religious organization which offers prayers and worship to God which deliberately exclude the name of our Lord and Saviour Jesus Christ, in whose name only is salvation to be found, is apostatic...'[16] 'Masonry is not so much a religion as a parasite on religion and a rival to the church...'[17] Anyone who takes God and the Bible seriously cannot but agree with this conclusion.

What can we do about it?

What practical steps should Christians and churches take concerning Freemasonry?

Convinced of the incompatibility of Freemasonry with biblical Christianity, Rev. Harry Woods urged the Free Church of Scotland to take the following steps:

- That the church issue a clear condemnation of Freemasonry...
- That those who are presently members of both the church and Freemasonry be asked to renounce their lodge membership, failure to do so being a disciplinary matter.
- That our people be warned against the errors of Freemasonry from pulpits...

  This is an important issue. We would not tolerate a man being a member both of our church and a Mormon temple. Why should we allow simultaneous membership of the church and a Freemason temple? ... The Word of God teaches the exclusiveness of

> the Christian faith and the forsaking of the temples of idols (2 Corinthians 6:14-18).[18]

There are encouraging signs that a number of other churches in Britain have implemented the measures proposed by Rev. Woods.

RELEVANT COMPARISONS

Freemasonry	The Bible
GOD	
New members, in their initiation ceremony, are introduced to God as the 'gaotu', that is, the Grand Architect of the Universe. They also learn another divine name, jhvh — a reference to Jehovah. At the top of the altar in the Royal Arch appears the 'sacred and mysterious name of the true and living God most High', namely, Jah-Bul-On, which is composed of the Hebrew 'Jahweh', the Assyrian 'Baal' and 'On' used in ancient Egyptian mystery religion in offering prayer to the god Osiris. Other titles of God include	'...and no one knows the Father except the Son and those to whom the Son chooses to reveal him' (Matthew 11:27). 'No one has ever seen God, but God the One and Only, who is at the Father's side, has made him known' (John 1:18). '...the mystery of God, namely, Christ, in whom are hidden all the treasures of wisdom and knowledge' (Colossians 2:2-3).

'Grand Geometrician' and the 'Great Overseer'. They claim to have the secrets concerning the 'lost name of God'.

BIBLE

The Bible is not a unique nor sufficient revelation from God. The writings of other religions, e.g. the Koran and the Vedas, are equally authoritative although in 'Christian' lodges usually only the Bible is used.

'Your word is truth' (John 17:17).

'Lord, to whom shall we go? You have the words of eternal life' (John 6:68).

CHRIST

Christ is totally excluded from this movement and they deny that he is the world's only Saviour.

'He who does not honour the Son does not honour the Father, who sent him' (John 5:23).

'For there is one God and one mediator between God and men, the man Christ Jesus, who gave himself as a ransom for all men' (1 Timothy 2:5).

SIN

While Freemasonry encourages decency, good works and civil obedience, it hardly mentions sin or repentance.

'...Jews and Gentiles alike are all under sin. As it is written: "There is no one righteous, not even one"' (Romans 3:9-10).

'...now [God] commands all people everywhere to repent' (Acts 17:30).

SALVATION

People are saved by their good deeds.	'Jesus answered, "The work of God is this: to believe in the one he has sent"' (John 6:29). 'But when the kindness and love of God our Saviour appeared, he saved us, not because of righteous things we had done, but because of his mercy...' (Titus 3:4-5).

THE GUIDE

Postscript

Summary of major Bible doctrines

Please note that the first four doctrines dealt with in the original work appear at the end of Volume 1 of this new edition, i. e. those dealing with the Bible, God and the Holy Trinity.

THE GUIDE

CHAPTER TWENTY

MAN: HIS CREATION AND FALL

A BRIEF HISTORY

What am I? Why do I behave as I do? Is there a purpose in living? These are some of the basic questions people are asking today. They are important questions, too. The true answers to these questions are given only by God and are found in the Bible. We shall consider briefly what the Bible says about man.

What am I?

Although it is popular to believe that man has evolved over millions of years from primitive animal life, the Bible teaches that man is a unique creation of God. For example, before creating man, the triune God is described as entering into divine counsel: 'Let us make man in our image, in our likeness…' (Genesis 1:26). On the other days of creation God said, for example, 'Let there be light,' or 'Let the land produce vegetation…' etc. However, on the sixth day God paused between two creative acts and the Holy Trinity enters into counsel before creating man. This illustrates man's uniqueness in creation.

Notice, too, that with regard to fish, birds and animals, etc., God created them 'according to their kind' (Genesis 1:21); that is, in a way typical and exclusive to themselves only. By contrast, man was created in the likeness of God. In some respects man resembles the animals. Both animals and humans need food and rest. They also have in common the senses of hearing, seeing, smelling, tasting and feeling. Nevertheless, there is an essential difference between ourselves and animals. Humans, unlike the animals, are God-related; they are made in the image of God (Genesis 1:26-27; 9:6; James 3:9).

What does it mean to be 'in the image of God'?

Just as God has personality, a mind, a will and the power to love and hate, so man has these characteristics of personality. God also has a moral nature; he hates sin and loves what is pure. Being made in the likeness of God means that all humans, despite sin, have a moral sense of right and wrong.

Furthermore, as God is spirit (John 4:24), man was created with a spiritual dimension so he can enjoy fellowship with God. Man is much more than a physical body or an aggregate of chemicals; he has a soul as well as a body (Matthew 10:28). Physical death is not the end of our existence as it is for animals; we shall live eternally after death in either heaven or hell.

We are now in a position to see some of the Bible's answers to our questions about human beings. What am I? I am a person created by God and radically different from the rest of creation. God's image is upon me and that is not true of animals. Is there a purpose for living? Yes, an important and satisfying purpose. God made man to enjoy fellowship with himself and to obey and glorify him (Ecclesiastes 12:13-14; Revelation 4:11).

Why obey?

Because we stand in a creature-Creator relationship to God, he has the authority to command us how we should live.

Adam and Eve were the first two persons God created. After Adam had been created, we are told that 'the LORD God commanded the man' (Genesis 2:16) not to eat the fruit of a particular tree. In this way God imposed his authority over man. God, of course, has every right to command us in this way. He is God. He is also our Creator. He rules the world he made. Despite sin, man remains under the authority of God and this is seen in many ways.

For example, God has given us consciences with a basic awareness of right or wrong and a sense of obligation to obey (Romans 2:14-15). God also exercises his authority over us through magistrates and governments (Romans 13:1-4), parents (Ephesians 6:1-4), husbands (Ephesians 5:22-33) and employers (Ephesians 6:5-9). The authority of God covers every aspect of our lives. God commands us what to do and how to live. Of course, people do not obey God in their lives and the Bible calls such disobedience sin (1 John 3:4).

Where did sin come from?

When God created Adam and Eve, there was no sin in their lives. They enjoyed and obeyed God in every detail. It was the devil, the first to sin (John 8:44; 2 Peter 2:4), who tempted Eve to eat the fruit of the forbidden tree. There was nothing in either Adam or Eve to make them sin (Genesis 2:15-25; 3:1-13; 1 Timothy 2:14). Sin came from without, yet Adam had the ability to obey or disobey God.

Adam our representative

What has Adam's sin got to do with me? Well, while Adam was an individual, historical person yet God also made him the representative of the entire human race. When Adam obeyed, we obeyed; when he sinned, we sinned, too. 'Therefore, just as sin entered the world through one man, and death through sin, and in this way death came to all men, because all sinned' (Romans 5:12).

THE GUIDE

CHAPTER
TWENTY-ONE

MAN IN SIN

A BRIEF HISTORY

There is not a single human being who is without sin. That is what the Bible says: 'There is no one righteous, not even one' (Romans 3:10); 'For all have sinned and fall short of the glory of God' (Romans 3:23).

What is sin?

It is important to understand what sin is. Sin is not confined to murder, rape or theft. In order to appreciate the nature and seriousness of sin, consider some of the words the Bible uses to describe it.

Lawlessness or transgression

In 1 John 3:4 we are told that 'Sin is the transgression of the law' (AV). The word 'transgression' or 'lawlessness' here means crossing over the boundary line into a prohibited area. Whatever the motive, the law is broken. This is a picture of our attitude towards God. By nature, we are rebels against God, his laws and his Word.

Sin disposes us to do what God prohibits. The Bible says, 'The carnal mind is enmity against God: for it is not subject to the law of God, neither indeed can be' (Romans 8:7, AV). The sinner is opposed to God and refuses to bow before God or submit to his laws.

Debt

'Debt' is another word the Bible uses to describe sin. In the pattern prayer given to the disciples, the Lord Jesus taught them to pray, 'Forgive us our debts, as we also have forgiven our debtors' (Matthew 6:12). In what sense is sin a debt? It does not mean, of course, that we owe sin to God. That could not be true, for God hates sin (Habakkuk 1:13) and does not want us to sin (James 1:13-15; 1 Thessalonians 4:3).

The word refers to the debt of obedience we owe to God. Perfect obedience is what God demands from us, but we are unable to pay God this debt we owe him. Sin is in that sense a debt and the 'wages of sin is death' (Romans 6:23).

Iniquity

This word means to twist or change the shape of something. After putting a piece of iron into the fire, for example, a blacksmith will hammer it into a different shape. A person suffering from rheumatoid-arthritis may find that his fingers become twisted out of shape.

Sin, too, is something which distorts and twists our lives (Psalm 51:9).

Missing the mark

One word frequently used in the Bible to describe sin means 'to miss' (Psalm 32:1; Isaiah 44:22; Jeremiah 31:34). The word literally means to have missed something, that is, we have wilfully missed God's purpose for our lives, preferring to live selfish, sinful lives rather than to glorify God.

This word also has the related meaning of missing the mark. The picture is that of a marksman who aims for a certain target with his arrow or gun but misses; or, perhaps, a person who fails to attain a pass mark in an examination. Similarly, sin for us means we have missed the mark of God's perfection and fallen well below the standards of his law. These standards are set out for us clearly in the Ten Commandments (Exodus 20).

There are three further things the Bible says about sin.

1. Sin is deeply rooted within us

Sin is not only something we do, like stealing or lying. These things, of course, are sinful, but we behave in a sinful way because we are sinful by nature. Let me put it in another way. Sin is not something we catch from other people, like influenza or smallpox. The reason is that sin is already within us. We were actually born in sin (Psalm 51:5). Our sins, then, stem from our sinful nature. 'For from within, out of men's hearts', said the Lord Jesus, 'come evil thoughts, sexual immorality, theft, murder, adultery, greed, malice, deceit, lewdness, envy, slander, arrogance and folly' (Mark 7:21-22). Sin comes from within our human nature. For this reason it is not enough to stop certain bad habits. That is like cutting off the top of a weed in the garden while the root is still left in the soil to grow again. God works differently. He goes to the root of all our troubles; he gives the believer a new nature and changes him from within. That is why the Lord Jesus told Nicodemus, 'You must be born again' (John 3:7).

2. Sin is extensive in our lives

Our actions, thoughts, desires, motives, will and affections are all influenced strongly by sin. 'The heart is deceitful above all things and beyond cure. Who can understand it?' (Jeremiah 17:9). 'Heart' here refers to the entire person, including mind, will, affections and desires. Just as some kinds of rash spread over the body so sin has spread into all areas of our lives. There is no part of our lives which is free from sin.

3. Sin is punishable by God

God is holy (Isaiah 6:3) and cannot ignore or tolerate sin. All sin is punished by God. There are different ways in which God does this but the climax is the sentence of unbelievers at death to hell (Matthew 25:41; Luke 16:19-31).

Is there hope for sinners? Yes. God has made a way of escape for us in Christ. God's own Son was 'pierced for our transgressions ... crushed for our iniquities ... by his wounds we are healed' (Isaiah 53:5).

THE GUIDE

CHAPTER TWENTY-TWO

THE PERSON OF CHRIST

A BRIEF HISTORY

It was a profound and searching question that the Lord asked his disciples at Caesarea Philippi: 'Who do you say I am?' Peter's answer was equally profound and true: 'You are the Christ, the Son of the living God' (Matthew 16:15-16). This was not speculation on Peter's part nor was it a merely subjective opinion. Far from it. The Lord Jesus commended the disciple for his answer but added, '...this was not revealed to you by man, but by my Father in heaven.' Not only did Peter speak the truth about the Lord Jesus Christ; it was God the Father who enabled him to make the confession concerning Christ's unique sonship with the Father.

As 'the Son of the living God', the Lord Jesus is unique but let us consider some of the biblical evidence for this fact.

His pre-existence

More than once, Jesus emphasized that he had come down from heaven (John 6:38). 'I am from above', he told the unbelieving Jews (John 8:23).

He did not begin to exist at the time of his birth. In fact he claimed, '...before Abraham was born, I am!' (John 8:58). Abraham's brief physical life had come to an end but Jesus, who existed long before Abraham, still exists as the timeless 'I am'. While praying for his people, the Lord spoke of the glory he enjoyed with the Father 'before the world began' (John 17:5).

His virgin birth

Although betrothed to be married, Mary was still a virgin. She was not guilty of pre-marital intercourse. No, she was a virgin who could say honestly to the angel, 'How will this be, since I am a virgin?' (Luke 1:34). The astonishing news, however, was that a virgin was to conceive and bear a son without the co-operation of any man. No wonder she asked, 'How will this be?' Mary was told that her child would be conceived through the power of God: 'The Holy Spirit will come upon you, and the power of the Most High will overshadow you...' (Luke 1:35).

The child born in a miraculous way to Mary was a special person. 'He will be great,' said the angel, 'and will be called the Son of the Most High... he will reign ... for ever; his kingdom will never end... [he] will be called the Son of God' (Luke 1:32-35). The Lord Jesus is distinguished from all others: he alone is the Son of God.

He forgives sin

The first words of the Lord Jesus to the paralysed man in Capernaum were, 'Your sins are forgiven' (Mark 2:5). Some of the Jews who heard the words were critical, for his words sounded like blasphemy. 'Who can forgive sins but God alone?' they replied. The answer of the Lord is significant in verses 9 and 10 and he healed the paralysed man so that they should 'know that the Son of Man has authority on earth to forgive sins'. The implication is clear: only God can forgive sins and, therefore, Christ in forgiving the paralytic underlined his own deity.

His equality with God

'I and the Father are one', claimed the Lord Jesus (John 10:30). More than oneness of purpose is intended here for the Jews were ready to kill Jesus 'because', they said, 'you, a mere man, claim to be God' (v. 33).

He is Jehovah

Did you know that Jesus is actually called Jehovah, a name only applied to God in the Old Testament? For example, the prophecy of Isaiah

40:3 was fulfilled in the work of John the Baptist. John prepared the way for Christ, who was the one Isaiah called Jehovah or Lord (see, too, Mark 1:3). Again, the description of Jehovah in Psalm 102:25-27 is applied to Christ in Hebrews 1:10-12. Isaiah also saw the glory of Christ when he saw the vision of God in the temple (Isaiah 6:1; John 12:41). In Zechariah 2:9-11 there are two persons described as Jehovah and in the opening verses of chapter 3 these two persons called Jehovah speak to each other! The unique claim of God in Isaiah 48:12 is applied to himself by Jesus in Revelation 1:8 and 22:13.

Yes, Jesus was God but also man. He needed to be the God-man in order to fulfil his unique mission.

He was man

No human being or angel could save us; only God could do so. But in order to represent us before God and save us, God the Son needed also to be man (Hebrews 2:17). There is another reason, too. As God, Christ could not die; it was in his human nature that he suffered and died for our salvation.

He was God

It was necessary for the Lord Jesus to be God. First of all, no human being or angel was qualified to save us or capable of doing so. Secondly, as a divine person, Christ was without sin and did not inherit original sin as we do. In addition, Christ had to overcome the devil, who is a powerful but evil angel. Furthermore, to save all God's elect from all their sins in all generations by his substitutionary sacrifice was a task only God could fulfil. Finally, only as God could our Lord's sufferings have an infinite value. Being man, Christ was able to die in our place and to procure our salvation; because he was God, his death has a value which is rich and infinite. It was as God, then, that the Lord Jesus humbled himself and stooped to become a man and a servant in order to die for our sins.

THE GUIDE

CHAPTER TWENTY-THREE

THE SACRIFICE OF CHRIST

A BRIEF HISTORY

One day while John the Baptist was preaching, he saw the Lord Jesus walking towards him and told the people, 'Look, the Lamb of God, who takes away the sin of the world!' (John 1:29). Again the next day, John stood with two of his disciples, then pointed to Jesus and said, 'Look, the Lamb of God!' (John 1:36).

A sacrifice

John's description of Jesus as 'the Lamb of God' would have impressed his audience. In the temple at Jerusalem a lamb was sacrificed every morning and evening. They knew they could not worship or approach God without sacrifice, for sin is hateful to the holy God. He must always punish sin. Somehow this wrath of God has to be removed before the sinner can approach God and enjoy his mercy. This could only be done through sacrifice: '...without the shedding of blood there is no forgiveness' (Hebrews 9:22). Accordingly, one of the first things a person saw as he entered the temple was the altar of burnt offering. Here the blood of the innocent lamb was poured out and its flesh burnt. All who approached God had to come by the way of this altar and sacrifice. There was no other way to God. Once the animal had been sacrificed at the altar as a substitute and punishment for the person's sin, then he or she could approach the holy God and receive forgiveness.

The people also associated John's words with the killing of the Passover lamb in Egypt. When the Egyptian leader finally refused to release Israel, God responded by killing off all the first-born males in Egypt. There was, however, protection for Israel if they sacrificed a lamb and sprinkled its blood outside their homes. Only the mark of the blood kept these families safe from death (Exodus 12). The apostle Paul tells us this was a picture of Christ's sacrifice on the cross of Calvary: 'For Christ, our Passover lamb, has been sacrificed' (1 Corinthians 5:7). It is only by the sacrifice of Christ that we can be saved from God's wrath and eternal death.

It was planned

All this was, of course, in the plan of God. Christ's birth and death were not an emergency plan suddenly put into operation by God. No, Peter says, he was 'foreordained before the foundation of the world' (1 Peter 1:20, AV). From eternity God had planned the death of Jesus (see also Acts 2:23).

All the details of his life, death and resurrection were also known in advance to the Lord Jesus Christ (Matthew 20:28; 16:21; John 10:11; 12:23-24; Matthew 26:26-46).

He was forsaken

It would be wrong to think that our Lord's suffering only began at Calvary. He suffered throughout his earthly life and in various ways. The climax of his suffering, however, was on the cross. After his arrest and trial before a Jewish court, Pilate, the Roman governor, agreed to his death even though he knew Jesus had done no wrong (John 18:38). The governor's decision was simply an attempt to please his Jewish subjects. It was not long before the Lord Jesus was led away for crucifixion at Calvary. The soldiers mocked him and wove a crown of thorns to put on his head. While he hung on the cross, people laughed and ridiculed him. The physical pain involved in this form of death was considerable.

But why was Jesus dying on the cross? He was not a criminal. Why did he die then? The Bible tells us: 'For Christ died for sins once for all, the righteous for the unrighteous, to bring you to God' (1 Peter 3:18). 'He was pierced for our transgressions, he was crushed for our iniquities' (Isaiah 53:5). 'The Lord has laid on him the iniquity of us all' (Isaiah 53:6).

In his body, the Lord Jesus bore the punishment of our sin. His sufferings were spiritual as well as physical. That is the reason why he cried from the cross, 'My God, my God, why have you forsaken me?' (Matthew 27:46). In the few hours the Lord was on the cross, he bore the wrath of God against our sin. To do this, however, involved the Saviour in forfeiting in his human nature the comfort and awareness of his Father's love and presence.

'It is finished!'

Christ did not suffer and die in vain. On the cross, he became our sacrifice and thereby removed all our guilt and punishment. All our sin was dealt with once and for all at Calvary. There is no need of any further sacrifice. 'It is finished,' declared the Lord Jesus Christ, (John 19:30). He died once and his sacrifice was complete and sufficient (Hebrews 10:14). Through this one, unique, atoning sacrifice, Christ has reconciled believers to God (2 Corinthians 5:19-21).

Our response

Christ himself, and only Christ, is the door to God and heaven (John 10:7-11). No church, no movement, no man, not even our best efforts can reconcile us to God. 'No one comes to the Father', said the Lord Jesus, 'except through me' (John 14:6). Our responsibility is to receive in faith, and rest upon, Christ alone for salvation. Faith is simply the hand we stretch out to receive Christ and his righteousness. Such faith is a gift from God (Ephesians 2:8-9).

THE GUIDE

CHAPTER TWENTY-FOUR

THE EXALTATION OF CHRIST

A BRIEF HISTORY

Jesus Christ was already dead when the soldiers inspected his body. A soldier cut open Jesus' side with his spear to confirm that he was dead (John 19:34). The Roman centurion in charge of the soldiers was impressed by what he had seen and heard of Jesus and immediately after his death remarked to the people, 'Surely he was the Son of God!' (Matthew 27:54; Luke 23:47). A man named Joseph obtained permission from Pilate to lay the body of Jesus in his own new sepulchre (John 19:38-42). The enemies of Jesus, however, were not satisfied. They placed soldiers to guard the sepulchre in case anyone tried to steal the body and then deceive people by saying that Jesus was alive (Matthew 27:62-66; 28:11-15).

The significance of the burial

The burial of Jesus was full of significance. For one thing, it was the fulfilment of a prophecy given 700 years earlier: 'He was assigned a grave with the wicked, and with the rich in his death' (Isaiah 53:9). Our Lord also prophesied that he would be buried (Matthew 12:40). In his burial our Lord surrendered himself to death and the grave. Just before he died, Christ commended his spirit to the Father (Luke 23:46) and was under the care of his Father.

On the third day, something wonderful happened. Some of the women went to the sepulchre but found the stone blocking the entrance had been rolled away and the body of Jesus was no longer inside. They were perplexed. Two angels then appeared to them and said, 'Why do you look for the living among the dead? He is not here; he has risen! Remember how he told you, while he was still with you in Galilee: "The Son of Man must be delivered into the hands of sinful men, be crucified and on the third day be raised again"' (Luke 24:5-7).

The Bible teaches that there is an inseparable relationship between Christ's death and resurrection (see, e.g. Philippians 2:5-11). As our mediator, Christ met all the demands of the law, paid the penalty of sin and obtained for us, through his sacrifice, life eternal. For his obedience in achieving all this for us, the Father rewarded Christ, our mediator, by exalting him.

The Bible distinguishes four ways in which Christ, our mediator, is exalted.

1. The resurrection of Christ

This was the first stage in the Lord's exaltation but attempts have been made to deny the fact that Jesus was raised from the dead. Was it just a hoax? The suggestion is absurd. If the enemies had stolen his body as a hoax, why did they not produce it when they tried to stop the disciples preaching Christ's resurrection? Or would the disciples have been willing to die just for a hoax? But did the Lord only swoon, not die, then revive again in the cold sepulchre? Remember, however, that the soldiers, as well as the disciples and Jewish leaders, were satisfied that Jesus was dead. It was in the interest of the Jews to be sure that he was dead.

There is firm historical evidence to show that the resurrection of Jesus Christ really took place. It is not just a myth or a fairy story. Think of all the people who saw and heard Jesus after his resurrection. Some of them, like Thomas, refused to believe until they had convincing proof (John 20:25). Paul also marshals convincing evidence for the resurrection of Jesus (1 Corinthians 15:5-8). Peter, James and the apostles saw Jesus alone after his resurrection. On one occasion about 500 people met and talked with Christ. In other words, the physical resurrection of Jesus Christ is historical and true.

The resurrection establishes beyond all doubt the truth of the Lord's teaching as well as his claim to be God. He 'was declared with power to be the Son of God, by his resurrection from the dead…' (Romans 1:4). By Christ's resurrection, the Father also indicated his approval of the Saviour's sacrifice for sin. Furthermore, the Lord Jesus promises to believers, 'Because I live, you also will live' (John 14:19; 11:25-26).

2. The ascension of Christ

The ascension of Christ is recorded in detail in Acts 1:9-11 (cf. Luke 24:50-51). Remember it was necessary for the Lord to ascend to the Father. As our mediator he was rewarded and entered into his glory in heaven: 'Did not the Christ have to suffer these things and then enter his glory?' (Luke 24:26). Christ had to enter heaven before the Holy Spirit could be poured out upon the church (John 16:7). When the Lord ascended, he also went as a forerunner to prepare a place for believers in heaven (John 14:2).

3. The session of Christ

When he ascended, the Lord Jesus was given a position of great honour at the right hand of God in heaven, and numerous Bible verses emphasize this point (Hebrews 1:3; 10:12; 1 Peter 3:22). What is he doing in heaven? As head of the church (Ephesians 4:15; 5:23; Colossians 1:18), he now actively rules over his church through the Word and Holy Spirit and also through pastors/elders whom he appoints to preach and rule in churches. Also it is from heaven that our Saviour builds and protects his church. This is not a difficult task, for all authority in heaven and earth belongs to the mediator (Matthew 28:18) and all powers are subject to him. Christ also prays for Christians (Romans 8:34) and sends the Holy Spirit to his church (Acts 2:33; John 16:7-15).

4. The return of Christ

The climax in the exaltation of Christ is yet to take place. Some time in the future, the Lord will return to this world. Christ has been once; that was 2,000 years ago. His purpose in coming to the world then was to save, and this he did by his death at Calvary. The next time the Lord comes, it will be to judge the world and to gather together and then glorify his church. There are many references to Christ's second coming in the New Testament and some of the more important ones are in Matthew 24-25; Acts 1:11; 3:20-21; 1 Thessalonians 1:10; 4:16-17; 2 Thessalonians 1:7-10; Hebrews 9:28 and 2 Peter 3.

How the Lord Jesus will return to the world

Personally

Jesus himself will return. He will not send a deputy or a messenger, not even an angel. 'For the Lord himself will come down from heaven' (1 Thessalonians 4:16). 'This same Jesus,' the angels told the disciples at the ascension, 'who has been taken from you into heaven, will come back in the same way you have seen him go into heaven' (Acts 1:11).

Visibly

The Lord Jesus emphasized this fact: 'They will see the Son of Man coming on the clouds of the sky...' (Matthew 24:30). His coming will not be secret or invisible, as the Jehovah's Witnesses teach. 'Look, he is coming with the clouds, and every eye will see him...' (Revelation 1:7).

Gloriously

His coming will also be glorious. The clouds will be his chariot and the trumpet will sound as the archangel heralds his coming. Christians already in heaven will accompany the Lord, while the mighty angels will surround him and execute vengeance on Christ's enemies (Mark 13:24-27; 1 Thessalonians 4:14-16; 1 Corinthians 15:23-28, 52). Christ will be revealed as King of kings and Lord of lords and all human activity will stop. The affairs of nations will come to an abrupt end.

Suddenly

People will be surprised by the suddenness of this event; many will be unprepared. Christ stressed this point (e.g. Matthew 24:37-51; 25:1-13). Only God knows when the return of Christ will take place. 'No one knows about that day or hour, not even the angels in heaven, nor the Son, but only the Father' (Mark 13:32).

When the Lord returns he will raise the dead (John 5:28-29; 1 Thessalonians 4:16), judge all people (John 5:27; 2 Corinthians 5:10; Matthew 25:31-46) then make a new heaven and a new earth (2 Peter 3:13) where only righteousness exists.

THE GUIDE

NOTES

NOTES

Chapter 1

1. *National Statistics (2004), Birth Statistics: Review of the Registrar General on Births and Patterns of Family Building in England and Wales, 2002, Series FMI, no.31.*

Chapter 2

1. 9th edition, p.327.
2. *The Guardian*, 22 January 2001.
3. D. B. Barrett, *Schism and Revival in Africa*, Oxford University Press, 1968.

Chapter 3

1. *South Wales Echo*, 19/5/01.
2. Allan Stibbs, *1 Peter*, Tyndale, p.94.

Chapter 4

1. See, for example www.cultnews.com.
2. http://news.bbc.co.uk/l/hi/world/americas/420935.stm

Chapter 5

1. *Sunday Times*, 19/12/99.

Chapter 6

1. *New Testament Theology*, IVP, 1981, p.436.
2. *Redemption Accomplished and Applied*, p.12.
3. *The Gospel According to John*, IVP, 1991, p.443.
4. D. M. Lloyd-Jones, *God the Father, God the Son*, Hodder & Stoughton, 1996, vol.1, pp.348-9.

Chapter 7

1. Letter, 11/06/96.
2. Letter, 11/06/96.

Chapter 11

1. Simon Tisdall reporting from Waco for *The Guardian Outlook*, 7 March 1993, p.23.

Chapter 12

1. *Western Mail*, 21 April 1993, p.8.
2. *Western Mail*, 28 April 1993, p.1.

Chapter 13

1. Zondervan, 2002.
2. *The New Mormon Challenge*, p.229.

Chapter 14

1. For confirmation of these facts, see for example, D. R. McConnell, *A Different Gospel*, Updated Edition, Hendrickson Publishers, 1995, pp.25-6.
2. The Unity School of Christianity as well as Spiritism are two examples.
3. McConnell, *A Different Gospel*, p.44.
4. *Science and Health*, p.109.
5. Rita Swan, *Cry, the Beloved Children*, Child, 1994.
6. Caroline Fraser, *The Atlantic Monthly*, April, 1995.

Chapter 15

1. *The Concise Columbia Encyclopedia*, Columbia University Press, 1995.
2. *The People's Chronology*, James Trager, 1994.

Chapter 16

1. *The Times*, 30 April 1978.
2. *The Rising of the Moon*, IVP, p.7.

NOTES

3. *The Times*, 30 April 1978.
4. Jacqui Williams, *The Locust Years: Four Years with the Moonies*, Hodder & Stoughton, 1987.

Chapter 17

1. www.netcentral.co.uk.

Chapter 18

1. www.scientology.org.
2. www.scientology.org/en_US
3. www.scientology.org.
4. www.beliefnet.com/story/80/story_8057_1.html)
5. www.scientology.org/en_US.
6. E-mail: Magoo44@att.net.
7. *Christianity Today*, vol. 27, no.4, p.32.
8. Newsweek, 6 December 1982, p.8.
9. *The Times*, 29 January 1986, p.12.
10. *Daily Telegraph*, 25 February 1986, p.9.
11. 'A Description of Scientology', www.scientology.org./en_US
12. www.scientology.org
13. www.xenu.net/roland-intro.html
14. www.modemac.com/cos/
15. www.modemac.com/cos/page2
16. www.beliefnet.com/story/80/story

Chapter 19

1. *Daily Telegraph*, 7 December 2004.
2. During 1985 the Methodist Church in Britain warned its members that 'There is a great danger that the Christian who becomes a Freemason will find himself compromising his Christian beliefs or his allegiance to Christ.'
3. Stephen Knight, *The Brotherhood*, Grafton Books, 1985, p.240.

4. Walter Hannah, *Darkness Visible*, Augustine Publishing Co.
5. Knight, *The Brotherhood*, p.246. Knight has a most helpful section detailing the history of the attitude of the Roman Catholic Church towards Freemasonry (pp.245-54), as well as the present confused position in which English Catholic bishops are more tolerant of Freemasonry than some of their colleagues in other countries.
6. David Yallop, *In God's Name, An Investigation into the Murder of Pope John Paul I*, Corgi Books, 1984.
7. Knight, *The Brotherhood*, pp.211-5.
8. Quoted in *The Brotherhood*, pp.131-2.
9. *Ibid.*, p.188
10. *Daily Post*, 27 May 1985, p.7. See also Narayan's book entitled *Barrister for the Defence*.
11. Knight, *The Brotherhood*, pp.49-63.
12. *Daily Telegraph*, 29 August 1984, p.13.
13. Knight, *The Brotherhood*, p.86.
14. *Ibid.*, pp.113-4.
15. *Banner of Truth* magazine, June 1986, Issue 273, pp.15-22.
16. Hannah, *Darkness Visible*, p.18.
17. *Ibid.*, p.30.
18. *The Monthly Record*, March 1987, pp.132-3.

INDEX

This index does not include biblical characters or doctrines, with the exception of the detailed treatment of certain aspects of biblical teaching in the 'Summary of major Bible doctrines'.

INDEX

INDEX